A Dear Son to Me
A Collection of Talks and Writings

Shefa

MAGGID

Adin Steinsaltz
(Even-Yisrael)

A Dear Son To Me

A COLLECTION OF TALKS AND WRITINGS

Maggid Books

A Dear Son to Me
A Collection of Talks and Writings

Maggid edition, 2011

Maggid Books
A division of Koren Publishers Jerusalem Ltd.

⬤ POB 8531, New Milford, CT 06776-8531, USA
& POB 4044, Jerusalem 91040, Israel

www.korenpub.com

© Adin Steinsaltz 2002
Published in cooperation with The Shefa Foundation
Translation copyright © The Israel Institute
for Talmudic Publications, 2002

The right of Adin Steinsaltz to be identified as the author
of this work has been asserted by him in accordance
with the Copyright, Designs & Patents Act 1988.

ISBN 978 159 264 282 3, *hardcover*

A CIP catalogue record for this title is
available from the British Library

Printed and bound in the United States

A Jewish family is like a circle – there is no end.

It is the responsibility of each generation to
make the circle larger and stronger.

Contents

Foreword

Traveling the world with Rabbi Steinsaltz allows plenty of time for conversation. One such opportunity came during a flight to Australia in 1993. I asked the Rabbi then, "You have been given so many titles: rabbi, philosopher, kabbalist, scientist, writer, etc. – but what are you really?"

His answer was short: "An educator," and he added: "This is what I've devoted my life to – reopening the world of Jewish learning to every Jew, especially to those who do not study, and whom you don't see in synagogue or in any other Jewish forum."

It is this philosophy that guides this collection of speeches and articles, from the late 1950s to this day. Rabbi Steinsaltz has written dozens of articles about a wide variety of topics – "Everything from cats to the Talmud," as he himself puts it – many of which have never been published. In addition, he has spoken to hundreds of Jewish communities around the world, and many of these speeches have been recorded and videotaped.

As a result, we have a sizeable collection of material from which we had to choose this unique collection. Selecting was no easy task, and I wish to thank Meir Hanegbi, Yehudit Shabtai, and Sue Jutkowitz for their assistance. The focus of this volume is – as its subtitle says – the people of Israel, the Jews. The book is divided into four parts: The Jewish people, the State of Israel, the Diaspora, and the Jewish individual. The theme that binds these four sections together is the Rabbi's profound love for each and every Jew, as well as his deep concern for the Jewish people and the land of Israel.

Except for the inevitable light editing, we tried, as much as possible, to preserve the Rabbi's voice, that changes according to the audience and the circumstances. I would like to thank Yehudit Shabtai for the great sensitivity with which she edited the material, and Gershom Gale for his fine style editing. Often, in order to retain the Rabbi's warmth and authenticity, we had to forego some of the conventions of editing – such as repetitions, or certain expressions that do not usually appear in print; but we felt a special need to transmit the material just like this to the Rabbi's friends and students, for whom this volume is especially intended.

Still, as the Rabbi says, "Once I submit a book to a publisher, it has its own life; I have no way of knowing what happens to every single volume. It's like shooting in the dark – you don't know if you hit or miss." This book, too, will surely have a life of its own, and we have no way of knowing whom it will reach, and who will be "hit" by it. We hope that it will indeed reach the hearts of its readers, and that it will also change something in their paths not only forward, but also upward.

Thomas Nisell
Jerusalem, September 2002

To the Jewish People

Chapter One

On Whom Can We Rely?

Some events are seen as historic turning points when they occur, but in retrospect are revealed to be much less significant. Other events may not seem so conspicuous, but create profound changes. I wish to focus on events of the latter kind.

During the past year, a number of important Jewish leaders have departed. They were leaders, not necessarily in the sense that the entire people followed them. But they were people whom everybody – both those who agreed with them and those who did not – was compelled to relate to in some way. They blazed a path, and even those who did not accept it recognized its significance. It could be said that they set the parameters of reality for all, and their absence emphasizes the tremendous problem of lack of leadership.

Indeed, the most strongly felt problem in the world today, in both the Jewish and non-Jewish world, is the lack of leadership. Who will lead, who will show the way?

At the end of Tractate *Sota* (49a–b), there is a saying of Rabbi Eliezer the Great:

From the day the Temple was destroyed, the sages began to be like scribes, and the scribes became like public officials, and the public officials like common people, and the common people are themselves deteriorating.

"The sages began to be like scribes." What do we expect of the sages, the leaders of the generation? New patterns, new paradigms. We ask for breakthroughs, for the paving of basic paths, the solutions to key problems. Instead, the sages become like scribes, the teachers of young children. They repeat what everyone knows. When they speak, they deal in small details, and solve problems that have already been solved. If they write books, they write anthologies and summaries. They are incapable of innovation because they are no more than scribes, teachers.

"And the scribes became like public officials." They cease to teach and become like policemen. A large part of the teachers' work in schools throughout the modern world is to impose order and discipline. In certain places, their function is simply to ensure that the students stay in their seats, do not talk, and do not disturb each other. In other places, it is to make sure they do not use weapons or drugs. There is no time left for learning, because the scribes have turned into guards.

"And the public officials [become] like the common people." The public officials mentioned in the Talmud are the officers and clerks of the court, whose function is to enforce order. Instead, these officials have become like the common people – simple, sometimes coarse, somewhat violent, somewhat delinquent. Instead of representing and enforcing law and order, they turn into yet another unruly, violent gang.

"And the common people are themselves deteriorating." The simple people are deteriorating, not necessarily in the economic sense, but in the spiritual sense – in what can be expected from them, in their gut reactions, in their basic demeanor. In this class – the lowest stratum of society – the general deterioration is indeed felt. Let me give one example. In a book written some 200 years ago, the author innocently writes: "Even the most frivolous, delinquent Jew at least wears a *tallit katan* and prays three times daily." Today, such a person is almost considered a man of stature.

This deterioration is an ongoing process of impoverishment to which one gets accustomed, and which one eventually accepts as the normal state of things. When my late father came to Israel as a ḥalutz, he had a dream that here, in this country, we would grow wings. That we would not only have a new earth here, but also a new heaven. Yet the people now inhabiting this land are gradually becoming *amei ha'aretz* (which in Hebrew means both "people of the land" and "ignoramuses"), a fact discernible in all aspects of life, from ways of expression to ways of conduct.

When I was a pupil at school, it was still possible to walk in the street and hear "juicy," vital, heart-warming Hebrew. Today, whoever listens to the language spoken in the street gets a strong sense of deterioration. And this is also true in matters that are more serious. There were times when no one locked their doors in Tel Aviv. Today, there is a theft in Israel every seven minutes. At the beginning of the century, one rabbi wrote: "Jews and blood – are there two more extreme opposites than this?" Today, a murder is committed or attempted every thirty-odd hours. This deterioration, then, is not just a matter of style. It affects the very foundations of life.

Rabbi Eliezer the Great adds: "And no one demands, and no one seeks, and no one asks." This poetic sentence seems to contain three synonyms. But there is a gradation here: He who "demands" does so with vehemence, requiring an answer and a solution. Less assertive is he who "seeks," who searches for and wants an answer, and least demanding of all is he who only "asks" a simple question. But everybody has become accustomed to the existing situation, "and no one demands, and no one seeks, and no one asks."

Rabbi Eliezer the Great concludes with the words: "On our Father in heaven."

This sentence, "On whom can we rely, on our Father in heaven," sounds like an expression of helplessness and despair. Imagine a sick person whose doctor tells him: "From now on, you would do well to rely on the Almighty." Such a person knows his situation is serious indeed.

However, this statement can also be read in a different tone – not as an expression of despair, but as a statement of fact, a piece of practical advice, a positive suggestion. And this has a number of aspects.

First, perhaps our generation would have preferred to find different leaders, but we cannot. We would have liked to find other teachers, other policemen, perhaps another people, but we cannot. There is a downhill trend, a deterioration. But there is one point that strengthens our heart: in the collapse of ideologies, theories, systems and politics, there is one thing which remains stable and on which we can rely – our Father in heaven.

And beyond that, the sequence of "sages, scribes, public officials, etc." implies a theoretical, emotional, and social structure in which we expect to lean on other people. Rabbi Eliezer's statement is a call to change direction. He says we have been leaning on sages and scribes and officials for too long. We have been leaning on them so much that we have forgotten our direct connection and direct commitment to the Master of the Universe, and this is why we are deteriorating. And he calls upon us once again to lean on the source of all things, our Father in heaven – or, in other words, to rebuild our direct and personal relationship with God.

In the Torah, we find several verses asking: "What does the Lord your God require of you?" (Deuteronomy 10:12). This is directed at each and every individual – not to the leaders, or to the audience, or to someone else, but to you. In the description of the making of the covenant between God and the Jewish people, this point appears in a verse directed to all generations. This special verse is phrased in a seemingly strange way: "The Lord did not make this covenant with our fathers, but with us, these here today, all of us alive" (Deuteronomy 5:3). This combination of words with the same meaning comes to give added stress. This verse says emphatically that the covenant is not of yesterday, and not with another people, but with us, each one of us, and not in a different time or place but "here, today."

This demand is very real. It requires the transfer of commitment, together with the burden and the effort, from the society to the individual. It prevents us from hiding behind any social, public, or historical structure, and it says: If we want a solution to the problem of deterioration, we are required to create a personal relationship with God, not only emotionally, but operationally – "We, here, today."

And this demand is difficult because our Father in heaven, unlike a policeman, accepts no excuses, and cannot be deceived.

In the period between the destruction of the Temple and the

coming of Mashiaḥ (the Messiah), when all systems break down and there is no longer anyone to follow, everyone will be called upon to start walking on his own, with all the multitude of commitments that this entails. Thus everyone ought to start saying: "The world was created for me" (*Sanhedrin* 37a). At the same time, if something immoral or unjust happens in the world, one must say, "It is my fault." If there is a child in this country that suffers, an adult who commits a crime, the responsibility rests not only on this or that government office: it rests on me. When one personally feels the pain of the existing problems, this creates a new set of attitudes. I no longer have anyone to lean on, and so I must establish a direct line of communication.

In other words, it is clear to us that there is darkness, and that we need light. Perhaps more than one lighthouse has been extinguished. So there is only one way. Each and everyone must light his own candle. If all these candles are lit, together they will create a great light, perhaps even greater than any other source.

In the saying "On whom can we rely, on our Father in heaven" there is, then, a hope, even a promise to the Jewish people. Not only that we have on whom to lean, but also that we are capable of making the transition from hiding behind others' backs and of beginning to assume personal responsibility for what others do, and for what they ought to do.

A great advantage enjoyed by the Jewish people is that the Almighty has not required us to resort to an intermediary. In a certain sense, each of us has a "hotline" to God Himself which we can pick up and say – "You." Yet we must remember that this phone also rings in the other direction; He turns to us from time to time and asks – "What are you doing?" This question was first directed to Adam – "Where are you?" (Genesis 2:9) and it goes on being asked to this very day.

This question is asked with added vehemence in a society that is not as united as it should be, and which breeds mistrust. Such a society must once again ask, seek, demand, and rebuild anew from the small contribution of each individual. Let everyone remove the dirt at his front door, and the entire street will be clean. Let everyone light the candle of his soul, and the land will be filled with light. Let everyone take one step forward and upward, and we will shake the entire world.

When God took our forefathers out of Egypt, He performed

innumerable miracles for them – the Ten Plagues, the Giving of the Torah, the manna, the quails, the Well. Yet the Tabernacle of the Lord did not come down in fire from the heavens, but was built from the contributions of each and every Israelite. Eliezer the Great speaks of the time prior to the coming of Mashiaḥ when he says: We do not know how the Temple will be built, but it is we, each and every one of us, who must contribute to its foundations. Everyone will give his stone, his small share. Two stones build two houses; three stones build six houses (*Sefer Yetzira*), and so on, ad infinitum. When these stones come together, The City of our God will be built.

And then, only then, will we be able to say that we do indeed have someone on whom we can rely – Our Father in heaven.

28 September 1994

Chapter Two

Heritage and Inheritance

The Jewish people today is at a critical stage in its history. Many of us believe – despite the horrifying assimilation rate – that the maternity wards can make up for the absence of study halls. Nevertheless, if we continue along this path, we are moving toward a non-luminous future, a future in which we will become like the Samaritans – a small, detached, insignificant sect. What is liable to happen to the Jewish community in Russia in the coming decade will happen to European Jewry within twenty years; to American Jewry within thirty years; and to Israeli Jews within fifty years. Russian Jewry is at the forefront of the battle because the situation there is the most severe. If we succeed in stopping the erosion in Russia – nay, if we can change the direction of the flow – it will be a sign that such change is indeed possible, and that we are not merely standing at the limits of our past, but moving toward a viable future.

I wish now to touch on a wider issue: the meaning of the term "Jewish heritage" and its significance for us today. I will begin with a verse at the end of Deuteronomy: "Moses gave us the Torah, the inheritance (*morasha*) of the congregation of Jacob" (Deuteronomy 33:4). Our sages (*Sanhedrin* 91b) say:

"Rabbi Yehuda said in Rav's name: If one withholds a *halakha* (= teaching) from his pupil, it is as though he has robbed him of his ancestral heritage, as it is written: 'Moses gave us the Torah, the inheritance of the congregation of Jacob.'"

This is a very powerful statement indeed. It does not address the question of whether or not we should teach Torah; rather, it says that the Torah is an inheritance for the entire Jewish people. We must not withhold it from its proprietors, and whoever does so commits a grave transgression. *Midrash Tanna'im* on Deuteronomy 33:4 says:

"Do not say 'morasha' (inheritance), but rather 'me'orasa' (betrothed). This comes to teach that the Torah is betrothed to the people of Israel. And whence do we learn this? From the verse (Hosea 2:21–22): 'And I will betroth you unto me forever… and I will betroth you unto me in faithfulness.'"

And *Midrash Sifrei* (on Deuteronomy, paragraph 345) adds:

"Do not say 'me'orasa' (betrothed) but 'morasha' (inheritance), which comes to teach that the Torah is an inheritance for the people of Israel."

Midrash Vayikra Raba (Vilna edition, 9:3) brings a story which shows how much the world has changed, and yet how much it has not. The tale speaks for itself.

"Rabbi Yannai was once walking on a road and saw a man with a most impressive appearance" – big, rich and dignified, whose paunch walked ahead of him. Rabbi Yannai did not know this Jew, but, given his attire and conduct, he assumed him to be important, scholarly and influential.

"So Rabbi Yannai said to him: Would you like to come to our house? The man replied: Yes. Rabbi Yannai brought him into his home, and gave him food and drink. As they were eating and drinking, he examined the man in his knowledge of the Bible, and found that he had none; he examined his knowledge of Mishna, and realized that he had none; his knowledge of *Aggada*, and saw that he had none; his knowledge of Talmud, and lo, he had none."

Thus it turned out that this impressive-looking guest, who bore himself as if he were a venerable rabbi, was a total ignoramus.

What, then, could Rabbi Yannai do? "He invited the guest to say Grace after Meals. Said [the guest]: Let Yannai recite grace in his own home." So Rabbi Yannai understood that his guest could not even say this blessing. "He told him: Can you at least repeat what I say? Said he: Yes. Said Rabbi Yannai: Instead of Grace after Meals, say: 'A dog has eaten Yannai's bread.'"

This is certainly an offensive statement, but this was how Rabbi Yannai felt. His guest "stood up and grabbed Rabbi Yannai, saying: My inheritance is with you, and you are withholding it from me!"

"What legacy of yours is with me?" asked Rabbi Yannai, puzzled. "He replied: I once passed by a school and heard the voices of little children saying 'Moses gave us a Torah, the inheritance of the congregation of Jacob.' They did not say 'the inheritance of the congregation of Yannai,' but 'the congregation of Jacob.'"

And this is how this story ends: Rabbi Yannai felt ashamed because he had become aware of his guest's true stature. The man's total ignorance was no reason for Rabbi Yannai to humiliate him. The Torah does not belong to Rabbi Yannai and his friends, but to the entire Jewish people. Therefore, the person who knows no Torah is not a dog; he is an educationally deprived person, a spiritual pauper who should be pitied, not abused.

"Said Rabbi Yannai to that person: What then has made you worthy of eating at my table?" I must assume that if you merit my company, you must have done many good deeds. "The man replied: Never in my life have I heard something negative about someone and run back to that person to tell him about it; and never in my life have I seen two people fighting without having made peace between them. Said [Rabbi Yannai]: So much civility and good manners are in you, and I called you a dog! And he applied to him the verse (Psalms 50:23): 'He appraises his path': he who assesses his actions is worth a great deal."

This person, who had no Torah, no Mishna, and no *Aggada*, turned out to be a giant in good conduct.

This story, which took place some 1,800 years ago, reveals a great deal about society, human relations and estrangement, and shows that none of these issues are new. But at the focus of this story is the reaction of the guest. This man had no knowledge whatsoever of the Jewish sources; he could not even recite grace after meals. Yet when told "Get out of here, you are a mere dog, I have nothing in common with you," he knew one thing: that the Torah is his inheritance, something which not even Rabbi Yannai could withhold from him.

Midrash Tanḥuma (*Vayak-hel* 8) adds:

> "When the Almighty told Moses to make the Tabernacle, he said about each and every item within: 'And you (singular) shall make' (Exodus 25:13, 17, 18, etc.); But when it came to the Ark, He said (ibid., 25:10), 'And they shall make.' Why? Because the Almighty commanded the entire Jewish people to make the Ark so that no Jew would ever be able to say to another: I gave a lot more for the Ark than you did, and therefore I have a greater share in it than you, while you gave only very little for the Ark, and therefore you have no share in the Torah. This is why the Torah was likened to water, as it says (Isaiah 55:1): 'Ho, everyone that thirsts, come to the waters.' Just as no person feels too shy to say to another, 'Give me water,' so no one should feel ashamed to ask someone lesser than he, 'Teach me.' And just as whoever wants water should drink for free, so whoever wishes to study Torah should study it without a fee, as it says (ibid.): 'Yea, come buy... without money and without price.' And why was the Torah given in the desert? To teach that just as the desert is ownerless, so too the words of the Torah are for whoever wants to learn."

Finally, *Midrash Sifrei* on Deuteronomy, paragraph 345, illuminates another reason why the Torah is called "the inheritance of the congregation of Jacob." Even an individual Jew who once learned Torah and then strayed to distant places is not ashamed to return, for he says: It is to my ancestors' property that I am returning. *Midrash Tanna'im* on Deuteronomy 43:4 likens this to a prince who sailed to far away countries. Even after a hundred years, he is not ashamed to return, for he says: "It is to the kingdom of my forefathers that I am returning."

"The inheritance of the congregation of Jacob" is, then, the inheritance of all Jews throughout the generations, in all their wanderings, however far off they may be.

From this sampling of sayings by our sages, we can see that these are not just heartwarming homilies about the relationship between the Jews and the Torah. Rather, a broad worldview is being outlined, one which is summed up in the *Zohar* as the threefold bond between "[the people of] Israel, the Torah, and the Holy One, blessed be He" (see *Zohar, Aharei Mot* 73a).

The threefold bond is also a national and social definition. It underscores the fact that the Torah is "the inheritance of the congregation of Jacob." The Torah is not the property of a certain group or brotherhood. In the Jewish people, there is no sect of "knowers" to whom alone the Torah was given. Rather, the Torah is for the entire Jewish people. Furthermore, the Torah, which is also called an "inheritance," is an ongoing legacy. No Jew is free to consider whether he wants it or not, nor is it for any of us to decide whether to take it or leave it. Rather, the Torah is the inheritance (*morasha*) of the entire people as a legacy (*yerusha*), as heredity (*torasha*).

This view also has practical implications. First and foremost, it is a matter of attitude. On the one hand, the fact that the Torah is "the inheritance of the congregation of Jacob" means that it is a legacy for my forefathers, for myself, and for my descendants. Even one who left this path a hundred years ago, and presently knows nothing about the Torah, can still return and reconnect himself with it, saying: "It is to my ancestors' property that I am returning."

On the other hand, no one can hold the Torah in his lap and claim that it is his own private property, or that it belongs only to his specific circle or group. For the Torah is the patrimony of the Jewish people as a whole, which includes each and every one of its members.

How was this inheritance taken from us? It got lost in the exiles, in the "desert of the nations," sometimes even in our own land. And it is my duty to return what was stolen from us to its owners, to all those entitled to it. This calls for a great deal of work, on both ends.

On one end are the recipients, who do not always know that they have such an inheritance. To use an ancient parable: a prince, born far away from his homeland, may not know that he is of royal descent, and is surely unaware that he has a great legacy in another country. What should this child do? He must learn about his estate; he must discover that there is a treasure awaiting him.

On the other end are the givers, or those capable of giving. The Torah is not something secret, or somebody's monopoly; on the contrary, we are commanded to make sure that it reaches the hands of every potential inheritor, all those who belong to "the congregation of Jacob." We must not deprive them of their legacy. Whoever tries to veil the Torah, or hide it, or build fences around it, separates his people from their heirloom, which is, and remains, theirs at all times.

This, then, is a twofold effort: of the child who grew up ignorant of his patrimony, and of he who holds any part of that inheritance and is capable of transmitting it. Both parties together must exert themselves to make the ends meet. Our great task is not to convert gentiles, but to proselytize Jews.

This heritage must therefore be transmitted and distributed, even to those who do not know it exists. One who holds in his hand even a tiny portion of this treasure has no right to keep it to himself. This is a direct, personal calling; it is not the responsibility of lawyers or of special institutions or organizations. It is the simple, humane duty incumbent upon me, who sees princes roaming the streets naked while I hold their plundered property in my hand.

To put things in proportion: the land of Israel is the Holy Land, the only land that is holy. Jerusalem is more sanctified than all the land of Israel, and beyond the sanctity of Jerusalem is the sanctity of the Temple Mount.

But above and beyond all this is the sanctity of the relationship between the Almighty and the Jewish people. This silver cord, this lifeline which links every Jew to his Creator, carries the sanctity from which all other sanctities derive. When one keeps this life-line intact, when one enables this flow of life to continue – this is where God is. Beyond that, He cannot be revealed.

The task of returning what has been lost to its owner is a very dramatic one. Sometimes one can only do a small part of it. Sometimes a person may begin, but not get to see the end. This is especially true because so many of the recipients are suspicious of the inheritance they are being offered. At other times, the paupers may have become accustomed to their poverty; they may have decided they do not want to be entangled with a great legacy. But whenever one has the privilege of returning that legacy, it is a powerful experience indeed.

There are still so many who need this, who cry out for this. And all of us, each and every one of us, can do something in order to weave this silver cord anew, to once again extend this thread of life.

25 September 1996

Chapter Three

Nationalist Fanaticism

T he Islamic regime in Iran is an example of the religiously fanatic governments that seem to have become a fashion in the Near East. Qaddafi in Libya, Khomeini in Iran, and others in the region are religious fanatics who change the entire structure of their countries in a frightening way.

Fanaticism, especially religious fanaticism, is frightening not only to those living under such regimes (especially to those who do not adhere to the same religious sect) but also to leaders of other countries. Religiously oriented rulers seem to walk in an entirely different world, a world in which many of the assumptions of modern civilization do not hold. The rules and conventions that provide the background for every other diplomatic and political movement seem to lose any meaning among these new leaders, who operate under a very distinct set of axioms.

Strangeness is the least of the reasons for the unpleasant feelings such rulers arouse. There are other, more substantial reasons. Sometimes the cruelty, even viciousness, of such regimes is shocking, even for a world that has accustomed itself to every kind of cruelty. But the biggest reason for fearing fanatic leaders is that they are led by irrational calculations that bring their countries, and sometimes the whole world, to destruction.

An ordinary political leader, even if he is dictatorial or mad, is somehow bound by rationality into taking or avoiding certain steps. But fanatical leaders do not seem to abide by any of the rational ways of the world.

This alarming situation has another side. Religious fanaticism, even with its strangeness and danger, also has some positive aspects. Because the fanaticism is religiously motivated, its rulers and leaders behave according to the code of their own spiritual world. There is a very strong, self-limiting factor in every religion, however fanatic it may be. This self-limiting factor is the religion's set of rules, laws and customs. Therefore, even in the Muslim world, some extreme movements that spawn semi-military sects and lead their followers into wars of conquest – such as the Mahdi in Sudan during the nineteenth century, and the Wahabis, who constitute the Saudi government of today – become quite politically moderate. This is largely because, after their initial success in war, their own ideology leads them to build some positive state or society.

A religion may be cruel, base, and objectionable, but it still has laws and rules that keep it within the bounds of its own goals. When one knows these laws, one can deal within their framework, and can bargain in their terms. Thus one may attempt to establish at least some kind of co-existence.

But the most important characteristic of the new fanatic Muslim regimes in the Near East is that they are not purely religious systems. They are, since their very beginning, a combination of religious fanaticism with modern, Western-style nationalism.

Western nationalism, while it has caused unspeakable disasters in its more extreme forms, is still able to balance itself with other powers and political views (not only in extreme fascist-like regimes, but even in most democracies). Western nationalism operates on a set of ideas that is primarily self-centered, because its only reason for being is to further the well-being of the state. More than that, from the time of Machiavelli, one thing has become more openly understood among national leaders: the state may maintain rules and order within itself, it may even adhere very strongly to such rules (democratic or otherwise), but in foreign affairs, it can employ any means to further its political aims. Truth, justice, integrity, the keeping of treaties and so on, are only sacrosanct under certain conditions; these "principles" are adhered to only as long as they further the interest of the nations that conceived them. The fact that there is some kind of balance, even peace in the world from time to time, stems from political necessity and considerations of one's own welfare. These rational considerations limit the Western state, and enable some rational inter-state relationships.

These two systems have defined limits and borders; the religiously fanatic state has no true political considerations but has a spiritual-religious code and self-limiting rules. The Western state does not have such a self-limiting system, but has an outwardly limiting system grounded in vital political considerations.

The Khomeini type of regime is more than a renewal of ultra-conservatism; it is a new political form, a nationalistic-fanatic system. This new system creates a state in which the leader and the government do not operate from any real political considerations; indeed, they are often driven by their beliefs into apolitical, counter-productive moves. But because their fanaticism is influenced by Western nationalism, the restrictive power of the religion is rapidly weakened.

As long as the rulers believe in their own religion, they are limited by it; but when they combine their own unrestricted religious aims with a political system that has no rules of its own, such as Western nationalism, they create the most terrible combination: "The Mad State." Such states are not restricted by external political pressure, because political necessities are not of supreme importance to them. At the same time, religious considerations are corrupted or destroyed by the Machiavellian notion that a state can justify any means it uses.

Extreme Muslim rulers (as in Saudi Arabia) sanction the execution of adulterers and the maiming of thieves, and may attempt to spread this gospel beyond their own country. But at the same time, their religion keeps them from aligning themselves with systems that are anti-religious, such as communist ones. Thus there is some limit to the behavior of these countries that makes them moderately reasonable. But this last restriction ceases to apply when the views of religious extremists unite spiritually with those of modern Western nationalism. Leaders of such religious-nationalistic hybrids write treaties, help and receive help from different, sometimes opposing, powers (such as Qaddafi in Libya), and then become so dangerous that there is almost no remedy but destruction.

Such regimes usually destroy themselves, either from the internal uncertainty that stems from the hypocritical application of rules and laws, or by waging war against powers that are too strong for them. But as long as they exist, these Islamic-Western hybrids are centers of a spreading malady, and may infect the entire geographical-cultural domain of Islam.

1984

Chapter Four

What Is a Jew?

A few years ago, there was a great commotion in the State of Israel (and consequently in other places) about the issue of "Who is a Jew." The impression was that the thoughts expressed addressed a central problem. In truth, however, the discussion did not go beyond the marginal definition – namely, who is or is not to be included in this category. Most of what was dealt with were borderline cases, the result being that the central issue – what is the essence of a Jew who is Jewish beyond doubt – was brushed aside. The different solutions offered for borderline cases were based on the universally-accepted definition of a "Jew," but the main issue was not touched.

"What is a Jew?" is an issue that occupies everyone who belongs to Judaism one way or another. Reaching clear decisions about it can determine the connection of those Jews – who are Jews beyond any doubt – to their nation, and it is therefore of decisive importance for the very essence and existence of the Jewish people. A comprehensive and meaningful definition can also determine if, and to what extent, "Jews" exist, and whether Judaism has any inner significance, besides being defined from the outside by anti-Semites of all kinds.

The very existence of such a definition – national, religious, or biological – can establish the meaning, and consequently the boundaries, of the Jewish entity. For many generations, this problem did not exist; the situation was clear and unequivocal. A Jew was whoever accepted, in faith and lifestyle, the totality of obligations imposed by the Jewish religion. Any serious deviation from this path, in thought or action, was seen as a parting with Judaism. This included not only Jews who converted to other religions.

From the halakhic point of view, apostates still belong to the Jewish people ("A Jew, even though he sinned, is nevertheless a Jew" – *Sanhedrin* 44a). Nevertheless, it was clear that whoever abandoned the Jewish religion was no longer a Jew de facto. Thus, even those who did not convert to other religions, but only deviated from the accepted, binding ways of halakha, were eventually torn away from the Jewish people, either intentionally or *ipso facto*.

Most of the heretic sects or those who deviated from halakha ended up outside the Jewish people. As a result, Judaism remained an essentially monolithic unit with ways of life determined by halakha, and an intellectual and emotional content created by a specific cultural heritage.

It must therefore be stressed that, both in terms of understanding Jewish history and in terms of its effect on the Jewish present, "Judaism" is a well-defined, unified concept.

From its very beginning, halakha has been connected with differences of opinion, some of which created divisions between sages and even between groups of Jews. However, despite all the disputes, and although dispute is a recognized component of halakha, there has always been a considerable amount of unity within Jewish law, and the same applies to principles of faith. The principles of Jewish faith were formulated in a relatively late period (the most widely accepted formulation was by Maimonides at the end of the twelfth century CE), though many sages to this day have been against formulating principles of faith of any kind. It is equally true that these principles of faith never had the binding authority of a "credo;" in fact, it is even unclear who wrote the Thirteen Maimonidean principles of faith printed in most prayer books.

Still, an analysis of the various Jewish sources shows that the principles of our faith are quite unified in terms of worldview and axioms. Examining even the most profound differences of opinion with the benefit of hindsight leaves one amazed as to how few there are.

This fundamental unanimity exists not because there is some central authority that decides what is permitted, what is forbidden, or what is true faith; rather, it is the result of the universal acknowledgment of a corpus of sources, and the acceptance of well-defined methods of interpreting and elaborating those sources.

Accepting the Torah as the foundation, and the halakhic Midrash as the only legitimate way of interpreting it, makes major differences between exegetical conclusions practically impossible, even when different parties try to emphasize those differences. The disputes between the House of Shammai and the House of Hillel – or, in a later period, between *Hassidim* and *Mitnagdim* – cannot be more than disputes about detail, or semantics.

This began to change in the nineteenth century, with the onset of the *Haskala*. More and more Jews ceased to accept the fundamental laws of Judaism, either partially or entirely, yet they did not convert to a different religion, and continued to see themselves as Jews. While in the nineteenth century such people were a small, sometimes even negligible, minority, by the 1930s they could already be considered the majority of the Jewish people.

How is the Jewishness of such people to be defined? If we are to apply definitions that were valid throughout most of Jewish history, then these people are either not fully Jewish, or completely non-Jewish. Again, it is important to note that halakhically speaking, there is no change in the Jewish status of such people. The majority of the Jewish people can be deemed, halakhically, "Jews who have sinned" – people who are still Jews, albeit with some halakhic limitations. Such a person's flaws, in faith and practice, do not affect his Jewishness. But still, the Jewishness of the majority of the nation today would not meet the definition that was valid throughout the generations.

This applies not only to those Jews who define themselves as completely non-religious, but also to most of the contemporary religious streams. The Reform, and to a certain extent the majority of Conservative Jews, cannot be included in the historical definition of essential Judaism.

The problem in their regard is not one of practical and halakhic differences, nor even in the acceptance or rejection of certain principles of faith. Throughout the generations, all the Jewish streams had a unifying element: all parties based their opinions on the same corpus of source material, and accepted the same methods of interpretation. It was thus always possible to argue, to debate. The debate may have been about whether or not to include certain books in the Bible, or about the interpretation of Biblical verses or passages from the *Zohar*, but whatever it was, all the disputants based their arguments on one and the same material, even if their conclusions differed widely.

Today, too, there are also such differences of opinion on various issues of halakha or faith; but the gap existing among today's Jews – even among the believers – is such that dialogue on a common basis is practically impossible.

From this point of view, only Orthodox Judaism (and this term applies here not to any specific political or religious stream, but to a way of life and to a worldview) can "pass" this Jewishness test.

Strange as it may seem, in the existing situation, only a small minority of the Jewish people can be considered truly Jewish. Hence the fundamental importance of the question, "What is a Jew?" Is there, or can there be, a definition of Jewishness that will be applicable to the majority of Jewish people today?

The problem of defining what a Jew is in our generation is not only in finding a formula that will be valid, and yet as precise as possible for the greatest possible number of Jews. An even more fundamental question is: in what way should such a definition be sought? And even more profoundly, should we look for a definition that will be based on the Jewish present, or on the Jewish past?

In other words, should the essence of Judaism be defined in a historical or in a non-historical way? The gap between the Jewish past and the Jewish present seems to make it impossible to find an historic solution.

Theoretically, it is possible to find characteristics, or ways of thinking, or abstract ideas that may define the essence of Judaism in our generation as it is, or at least as one can visualize its future development. But is it indeed possible to find a definition of the essence of the Jew that is detached from Jewish history?

The role of history in the life of the Jewish people is different from the role it plays in the life of all other ancient nations. In a certain sense, the past has a unique significance in terms of Jewish self-perception. All other nations, or well-defined national units, have various elements that reflect their uniqueness and turn them into national units: a homeland, a common language, a history, a common origin or a shared past. The entire Jewish people of today, however, has no geographical homeland; its original language is often only the language of prayer and study, not the language of daily life; and because the Jewish religion has been abandoned, Jews no longer have a shared culture, since Jewish culture is the totality of the expressions of the Jewish religion.

Of course there is a Hebrew culture, perhaps even a secular Jewish culture; but it is not the culture of the entire Jewish people, and it is not meaningful for the people as a whole. Hebrew literature, for instance, nourishes only residents of the State of Israel and Hebrew speakers. It is also difficult to say there is a "Jewish race"; even the anti-Semites did not manage to find any specific Jewish racial features. Geographical dispersion, on the one hand, and the acceptance of proselytes on the other, have slowly blurred the common racial origin.

The issue of proselytes is of special importance, for even without calculating the precise percentage of proselytes and their descendants in the Jewish people, their very inclusion and amalgamation precludes the existence of "a Jewish race." Hence, the shared Jewish past plays a major role in the definition of Judaism. Or, to put it even more emphatically: Jewish history is the Jewish people's homeland.

It must be stressed that this is a purely national definition, because the religious definition is largely ahistorical. As Rabbi Sa'adia Gaon puts it: "Our nation is a nation only in its Torah;" and since the Torah is not seen as a cultural-historic event, a Jew is whoever accepts the Torah as it is in the present; it makes no difference what his past was, or what the history of Jewish culture was up to that point. Seeing Judaism from more than the religious-halakhic point of view is, then, what forces us to give it an historical definition. In other words, any definition of "What is a Jew" that is not founded on the Jewish past will not only be unjustified historically, but will be meaningless in terms of the present. Any definition of Judaism, even if it deviates broadly from the clear and simple concepts of the past, must be rooted in that past. It may still be possible to reduce the essence of Judaism to a definition that can be more meaningful in the present, yet such a definition must nevertheless contain the entire past.

A Minimal Definition

So the problem of finding a meaningful definition of what a Jew is nowadays, is the problem of finding a minimal definition of Judaism – or at least a definition more limited in its demands than the Orthodox definition that has been meaningful until now.

The Talmud provides a sort of precedent for such a definition: "There are 613 commandments in the Torah; came [King] David and reduced them to eleven (see Psalms 15); came Isaiah and reduced them to six … came Micah and reduced them to three … came Habakkuk and reduced them to one, as it says (Habakkuk 2:4): 'the just shall live by his faith'" (*Makkot* 24a). At first glance, it seems that we have here a similar movement: 613 commandments that are reduced to a less demanding framework: the eleven commandments of King David, etc. One may see a similar trend in the famous reply that Hillel the Elder gave to the man who wanted to define a single principle that encompasses the whole Torah: "What is hateful to you, you must not do to others – this is the whole Torah" (*Shabbat* 31a); "Love your neighbor as yourself: Rabbi Akiva says: 'This is a major principle of the Torah;'" "Ben Azzai says: 'This is the book of the generations of man' – this is an even greater principle" (*Sifra, Kedoshim* 2:4).

All these sayings may be perceived as a search for a more limited kind of tradition, one that can encompass a greater number of people.

But if one looks more deeply, one will see the many difficulties that this entails. A closer look into the sources will reveal that, in fact, everyone agrees that the text is not trying to reduce the validity of the 613 commandments. What all these sayings are trying to do is to seek a common denominator for them.

The problem about these sayings is not in their intention, but rather in their practical application. Take, for instance, the broadest definition, that of Psalm 15, with its eleven commandments: "he that walks uprightly, and works righteousness, and speaks the truth in his heart; he that backbites not with his tongue, nor does evil to his neighbor, nor takes up a reproach against his neighbor; in whose eyes a vile person is condemned, but he honors those who fear the Lord; he who swears to his own hurt, and changes not; he who puts not out his money to usury, nor takes bribe against the innocent." These are all wonderful things, things that may well provide universal guidance for all times. But this is also their major weakness: they are so very general that they no longer bear any meaningful uniqueness.

Various modern Jewish streams that sought to operate on the basis of similar understandings (and theoretically, there still are such people in the Jewish present) ended up with a very flimsy and unconvincing set of religious or moral norms.

The main flaw of "Christianity without a cross," as such approaches have justly been termed, is not their closeness to Christianity; it is more fundamental than that. The flaw is that such approaches have no definite content. In other words, a definition that will be satisfactory and relevant for the majority of the Jewish people nowadays is most likely to be blurry to the point of insignificance. This applies to most of the non-religious Israeli attempts to find a minimal way of defining the Jews in the State of Israel, as well as for defining "a light unto the nations" in such a general way that it no longer has any meaning of its own, let alone being a light unto anyone else.

"Making the desert bloom," or "creating a socialist society," or "faith in Redemption," even when joined together, still do not create something of any worth. This has always been the fate of such searches for definition. For instance: basing all the commandments on "love your neighbor as yourself" surely grants this commandment a unique flavor; but detached from the 613 others, it is general to the point of meaninglessness.

The common denominator to the dozens of attempts to find such a definition for Judaism is an understanding that Judaism (in this indefinite sense) is something that does not have any inherent content. Such definitions not only lead to "liquidating" conclusions (because something that has no content is not worth keeping); most are essentially destructive, because they try to ignore whatever is unique and distinctive. In fact, they want to have nothing unique or distinctive about them, and therefore try to have as little specific significance as possible.

The conclusion is simple, though it may seem strange: in order for the minimum definitions of "What is a Jew" to have some significance, and not be merely meaningless chatter, they must contain, prominently, the point of Jewish uniqueness; they must speak about what makes a Jew different from other people. A definition of Judaism based on the 613 commandments does not have to stress that it is Judaism and not Buddhism. In order for reductive definitions to have some significance and relevance, they must be based on Jewish uniqueness in addition to their wider content. Phrased in the most general way possible, such a definition will be something like: Judaism is … a certain idea, a certain set of beliefs, etc. – *so long as Jews are concerned.*

In fact, all the definitions of what a Jew is that try to be as inclusive as possible share a common assumption that we are speaking about Jews. Whether they deal with the present or look to the future, they must acknowledge a connection to the Jewish people. It is therefore essential to have an understanding of the Jewish national bond throughout the ages in order to understand what Judaism is at any given time.

Beit Ya'akov – the House of Jacob

What creates the bond within the Jewish people? This question does not have a simple answer. We have already pointed out how difficult it is to see the Jews as a nation in the ordinary sense of the word. Since the destruction of the Second Temple, and possibly even since the destruction of Samaria, the majority of the Jewish people does not reside in its land or shape its own political life. From the purely political point of view, the Jewish history of the land of Israel is the history of the Jews of the land of Israel only. In the course of the generations there was surely a strong bond and intense cooperation between the Diaspora and the land of Israel, but this cooperation itself raises questions about the nature of the bond. The wondrous link between Jews throughout the world –

whose "un-normal" state was already recognized in olden times – and the land of Israel, still exists, to a lesser or greater degree.

Haman's definition, "There is a certain people scattered abroad and dispersed among the peoples in all the provinces of your kingdom, and their laws are diverse from those of every people. Neither do they keep the king's laws" (Esther 3:8), is quite ancient. Even back then, people could not understand the essence of this "people." But defining the Jewish bond as purely religious, and seeing Judaism as a religion and nothing more, is not enough.

It should be stressed that throughout the generations, the prevailing Jewish view was to leave the Jewish religion to the Jews. There were some exceptions, though; in certain periods there was a tendency for large-scale [forced] conversions to Judaism, but in most periods, we recoiled from such action. This means that the religious aspect of Judaism, as important as it may be, has to do only with Jews. Nevertheless, there was no objection to accepting proselytes from any people or race. There is, then, no "pure" Jewish race, and maintaining racial purity is not, in any way, a fundamental component of Judaism.

Despite all of the above, there is an original Jewish way of looking at what binds all Jews together. This is meaningful not only in terms of explaining the Jewish past; it also gives meaning to basic assumptions about "who is a Jew," and is significant even today. This way of looking at things holds that the Jewish people is not, properly speaking, a nation, but a family. "Beit Ya'akov," "Beit Yisrael" ("The house of Jacob," "The house of Israel"). These are the most prevailing appellations of the Jewish people, and indeed express this familial bond. A Jew is linked to his people not merely by cultural bonds, or by the existence of a geographical homeland. Belonging to a family is not voluntary; one does not choose one's family, nor is one free to rid himself of it. A person may dislike his family members, and even act willfully against them, but he is unable to sever his essential bond with them.

The idea behind the talmudic saying (*Sanhedrin* 44a), "A Jew, even though he sinned, is nevertheless a Jew," now becomes much clearer. The Jew's connection to the Jewish family, the house of Israel, cannot be nullified.

The Jewish religion, too, cannot be seen as a religion in the broader sense – namely, an expression of eternal, universal truths. This does not mean that Judaism contains no elements that may be meaningful for other peoples; but in its entirety, it is the way of life of the house of Israel, the pattern of behavior for the house of Jacob. The Jewish religion, then, is not a religion that happens to be practiced by Jews; it is the special religion of the members of the Jewish family. Hence also the lack of intentional missionary activity. The unwillingness to convert others is not an expression of arrogance; it is simply an attitude based on a common, uniting family bond that defines specific ways of life. Conversion to Judaism is therefore also seen as a joining to the special Jewish family, reminiscent of joining a family via marriage. The attitude to proselytes – a combination of sympathy, closeness, and a certain amount of suspicion – did not grow from a specific ideological background; it stems from emotions that are parallel to those that a family harbors toward a stranger that joins its ranks.

Identifying the unifying bond of the Jewish people as a family bond, rather than as a national bond, is not just a matter of terminology. The essence of the family bond is different, theoretically and emotionally, from any other kind of human tie. The family bond is primitive, essentially irrational; it is not based on any specific spiritual conception, and expresses only the sense of mutual belonging. Its primitive, irrational nature doesn't make it less intense; on the contrary, the family bond is the closest, most fundamental tie, as well as the bond that is the most difficult to undo.

The perception of the Jewish national bond in these terms is reflected, for instance, in the contempt for apostates felt by every Jew, even an atheist. This is similar to the emotion that family members harbor toward those who leave the family; they cannot simply accept it as a fact. It is impossible to sever the familial bond; but the desire to do so arouses a feeling of disgust.

What is the nature of this family bond? Contemplating the process of becoming a proselyte is a key to understanding the intra-Jewish relationships. While one who is born Jewish is automatically a Jew, becoming a proselyte requires one to be admitted into the house of Israel, a sort of adoption process. There are certain laws that set proselytes apart from the rest of the house of Israel, but these have to do only with intra-family divisions (e.g., the laws that set the tribe of Levi apart from the rest of the tribes). Apart from that, the proselyte, unlike the *ger toshav* (partial proselyte) is not merely an annex to the house of Israel, he becomes an integral part of it. He joins the family.

When and how is this act of joining accomplished? According to Judaism, "a proselyte is like a newborn baby" (*Yevamot* 22a), who leaves behind all his past relationships. Indeed, not only the national and racial bonds of the proselyte are considered null once he becomes Jewish, but also the biological links with his former family.

It should be stressed that the religious rites of conversion (circumcision and immersion in a *mikveh*), with all their halakhic importance, are not a sacrament of rebirth. Circumcision and immersion are independently existing Jewish commandments that bear their own specific meaning (unlike the idea of rebirth inherent in Christian baptism). The determining factor, without which the rite of conversion cannot become valid, is the desire to join and unite with the house of Israel, with all this entails. The proselyte becomes a Jew by his very desire to take Judaism upon himself.

In other words: the "Jewish family" is an ideological, not a biological one (and indeed, a proselyte is not the "son of Jacob," but the "son of Abraham"). The Jewish people is an ideological unit in the form of a family; a unique unit indeed, but also one that is defined through that uniqueness.

The saying of our sages, "your father – this is the Almighty; your mother – this is *Knesset Yisrael*" (*Zohar* II, *Parashat Yitro*, 85a) is neither a figure of speech nor a displaced theological formulation; it is a somewhat poetic description of the essence of the Jewish bond. The Jewish people is a family, and its members are brothers and sisters, children of one father. Yet although Abraham, Isaac and Jacob are the fathers of the Jewish race in the biological-historical sense, they are not the fathers of the Jewish family; the Jewish familial bond is created not by them, but by the "fatherhood" of the Almighty.

There seems to be no better way of expressing this idea than in the words of the prophet: "Doubtless, You are our father; though Abraham be ignorant of us, and Israel acknowledge us now: You, O Lord, are our father, our redeemer, Your name is from everlasting" (Isaiah 63:16).

This, then, is not a theological definition; "You are our father" is not a pious expression of religious fervor, but a quasi-biological statement. Jewish faith and the relationship to God are not abstract or "religious" in the same way that they are in other religions. The very relationship itself is the basis for Jewish togetherness. The religious attitude – what is commonly called "the Jewish religion" – is therefore a network of close father-son relationships and family rites. Beyond being a system of faith and beliefs, it is the maintenance and affirmation of the Jewish "familial bond."

These definitions are, of course, formulated in religious Jewish language, and are therefore easily refutable: What about Jews who do not fulfill the commandments? And what about Jews who do not relate to God in this way? And what about Jewish atheists, who negate God's existence altogether? But the Jewish bond is not dependent on accepting ideological fads: rather, it is a "familial bond," rooted in totally different strata of the soul. A son does not have to know the essence of fatherhood; he may even deny the existence of such a relationship, or the existence of the father himself – and still, he is a son.

Thus, while the ideological explanation may not be acceptable to some Jews, the familial bond continues to exist, even in a non-conscious way. Hence this fundamental national trait of being "a kingdom of priests and a holy nation" (Exodus 19:6) – that commitment to be a *kohen*, an envoy for a ritual of holiness, of redemption, of sublimity, in all the different forms and shapes they may take in the course of time. It is that sense of duty and exaltation that comes from being "sons of the living God" (Hosea 2:1) that appears in a myriad different forms, yet with one essential feature.

Hence the mysterious, wondrous, sometimes irritating sense of mutual binding that is enhanced in times of crisis. For these are the times we are called upon to figure out who we are and where we belong, the times when every member of the Jewish people feels that he is a son, and that he really belongs together with all the other sons.

Molad Journal, 1970

Chapter Five

Auto–Anti-Semitism

Strangely enough, anti-Semitism and complete devotion to Judaism have much in common. One does not have to dig too deeply into the soul to find the connection between love and hate. Simply put, both anti-Semites and devout Jews agree on one basic idea – that there is something uniquely significant about Jews.

For most people, a category of human beings who constitute less than half of one percent of the population does not deserve so much attention. Only Jews and anti-Semites think the Jews are so special, so important, that they should be thought about until it becomes almost an obsession. Indeed, the paradoxical fact remains that the most fervent believers in the chosenness of the Jewish people (even if without any excess of love) are precisely the most fanatical of the anti-Semites.

The odd connection between anti-Semitism and devout Judaism is one of the explanations for Jewish self-hatred, which includes everything from exaggerated self-criticism to fierce anti-Semitic sentiments. Among the psychological derivatives of the deep faith (irrational and often not conscious) that Israel is the Chosen People, there is a tendency to excessively severe criticism. What would be considered normal and even correct for others is inexcusable for the Chosen People.

When this self-criticism becomes overly rigorous, it makes one forget the primary element that was at its source, and it can become a sick antipathy – "auto–anti-Semitism."

Such self-dislike or even self-hatred is certainly not an unfamiliar phenomenon; many suffer from it to some degree. But the fact that this is so common among Jews in relation to Judaism, and especially among Jewish intellectuals, would seem to indicate that there are other factors involved. One of them seems to be the Jewish talent for imitation, cultural imitation in particular. This talent, which is an important survival tool for any weaker element in society, can extend far beyond merely pretending to be like the other, resulting in a genuine internalization of the values and ways of the other – a full identification. Indeed, so powerful can such an imitative urge become that it often functions without any positive feedback from the environment. Even when members of the surrounding society are antagonistic and unreceptive, the Jew will nevertheless often strive to be like them.

This imitative drive is compulsive and works on every Jew in an alien environment. But it is overwhelming for a Jew who knows nothing of Judaism. In such a case, the alien identity takes over completely, and the person or group is left without any vestige of true identity.

Yet in spite of this apparent loss of identity, Jewishness does not altogether disappear. A certain residue lingers, at least in the unconscious. Even the Jew who in terms of his awareness has become an inseparable part of a different culture is able to cherish a belief in the special importance of the Jewish people. He may also believe, however, that this importance is accompanied by a number of excessive demands. And the combination of these two elements – alienation from Judaism and an unrealistic understanding of what it means to be a Jew – easily leads to a certain amount of suspicion, hostility, and even hatred.

These antipathetic feelings create the sickness known as xenophobia – a fear and loathing of the "other." When such feelings are accompanied by an idea that the stranger, the object of repugnance, is somehow important or possessed of more than ordinary powers, such feelings crystallize into their most poisonous form – anti-Semitism.

At the same time, there is something ambivalent about anti-Semitism: anti-Semitic hatred also contains an element of envy, and even admiration. This mixture (in addition to other factors, such as broader views of life and culture) makes anti-Semites feel somewhat ashamed and apologetic.

The only ones who are free of such ambivalence are the Jews. When a Jew experiences a deep aversion to his Jewishness, he does not feel any need to be ashamed of his antipathy or apologetic about it. The fact that he is a Jew gives him the "right" to hate without feeling blameworthy.

Only he can be, in heart and soul, an auto–anti-Semite.

Unknown date (probably 1970s)

Chapter Six

The Rebbe's Century

We are celebrating the one hundredth year since the birth of the Lubavitcher Rebbe. One hundred years is a long time, which means – many changes, in many ways. It is a significant number in Jewish lore, because one hundred years marks a full cycle of life. One hundred years also defines a century, and I want to give it the recognition it deserves. I want to speak a little about that century, the century of the Rebbe.

The Rebbe's century was a truly astounding time. The world has changed in this century more than in the thousand years before, perhaps even the two thousand years before. In the sphere of geopolitics, the past hundred years witnessed numerous earth-shaking revolutions. Totalitarian dictatorships in Russia, Germany, Italy and Spain emerged and grew and achieved hegemony – and all of them collapsed. The map of the world changed tremendously: Europe, Africa, and Asia changed their faces. So much happened, including two world wars that shattered the planet.

There were changes in thought and knowledge. The new disciplines of psychology and psychoanalysis made a lasting impact on our culture. Abstract art, new forms of literature, and computerization brought entirely new images and ideas into the human experience. Our

new grasp of biology has brought about a tremendous shift in our understanding of how we change, and of the changes we generate. The theory
of relativity was a remarkable insight, irreversibly changing the world's
perception and understanding of itself. The century begat the atom
bomb, while our understanding of biology created genetic engineering.

These achievements, and so many others, hover over us as threats
and opportunities.

Taking a look at Jewish life, we see that within this century, it has
undergone three major transformations. The first unfolded slowly, and
its significance was not immediately evident. Following an extended
period in which the Jewish people had been more or less religious and
observant, a clear movement away from orthodoxy began. By the end
of World War I, most Jews were non-observant. This is a huge change.

The second change was brought about by the Holocaust. The
Shoah killed the core of Jewish life: men, women and children who were
the most vibrant, animated elements of the Jewish people. Six million
of them – or more – were killed.

And then there was the establishment of the State of Israel:
another unprecedented event, another tremendous change.

All these things represent dramatic alterations in the history and
life of the Jewish people; nothing like them had happened in the previous thousand years.

So the political world changed, the intellectual world changed,
and the Jewish world changed.

The Rebbe did not just live in the century in which these events
occurred. The Rebbe participated, at various levels and in different ways,
in many of them. He survived the pogroms in Russia as a child, was a
young man at the time of the Russian Revolution, and escaped from
Europe during the Nazi regime. His knowledge and understanding of
what was happening in the world were unique. One must remember that
the Rebbe could draw on vast stores of both spiritual and scientific wisdom: on his mastery of physics, biology, literature, and human nature.
The Rebbe was a part of all those changes, and he was also a person who
created and worked within them. He lived through the most fascinating,
frightening, and changeable time.

The Rebbe lived in the most difficult of times, yet he was always able to forge ahead. The Rebbe was not just aware of many of these changes; he predicted some of them.

But we must go one step further. Of course, the Rebbe was aware of the past – his own past, the past of his people, and the past of humanity. But with all that, he was always a man of the future. If you read through his many writings, you will find hints here and there about the past, but the focus and direction are on the future. He sometimes spoke about what had happened, but more often about what should happen, what will happen. Some people thought of him as a symbol and a picture of the glory of the Jewish past, but this is an error. In many ways, he was a man of the next century, a man who belonged far more to the future than to the past. And this will explain what was so very important to the Rebbe in his last years.

The Rebbe watched the world and felt so much happening, so much quivering and shaking, but he did not see these developments as final effects. He saw them as tremors preceding a big upheaval. The Rebbe saw all the change and distress as labor pains that herald an impending birth. And that was what the Rebbe had in mind when he talked about Mashiah.

The Rebbe spoke about Mashiah because he saw the past, the century he lived through, as the preparatory rumblings before the huge upheaval. This is what he tried to tell people. This is the message he tried to communicate. As the years passed, he became more and more emphatic about the idea that Mashiah is about to come. He saw it not only through a heavenly vision; he perceived it in the way the world was moving, in the changes he had witnessed. He saw the movement, the suffering, and the pain as heralds of a major event, a major change, and that change is the arrival of Mashiah.

Clearly, the coming of Mashiah is not a mere happening within the world. It is far more important, far more profound. In the words of the Prophets, the coming of Mashiah signifies the end of days – that is, the end of history. It marks the beginning of a completely new era, an era so new that nothing in the past is parallel or connected to it. Mashiah will change history permanently, change human life permanently, and usher in a future that will be very different from the past.

The Rebbe was not just making conversation about Mashiah, and

39

he was not just talking about a prophecy that he wanted to preserve. The Rebbe spoke about Mashiaḥ because he understood that his coming is a process in which we must be both active participants and passive beneficiaries. It is a dual process, like birth, where you cannot really point out what part comes from Above and what part comes from below, from the inner workings of the human body.

This synthesis is what the Rebbe referred to when he spoke about Mashiaḥ. Therefore, the Rebbe did not see "Mashiaḥ" as a mantra to say six times or ten times a day to overcome difficult moments. For the Rebbe, Mashiaḥ was something to work on, to fight for. That is because we are built and our history is built, from the very beginning, as the prelude to the end of days. We are not working toward the end of human life, or to the end of earthly existence, but to a tremendous change in all of that. So we must not only speak about this process, but prepare for the events that will signal its completion.

In this context, let me address the Rebbe's "legacy." One should not use that word in talking about the Rebbe. He did not leave a legacy. The Rebbe left marching orders. This is an entirely different concept. The Rebbe did not just leave a collection of books, videos and speeches. He left a task to be completed, and the books and other resources provide the understanding that will enable people to carry it out.

I will try to outline some of the ideas that are in those orders, properly and correctly, and render his lofty words in simpler, more down-to-earth language. I believe that this is not just a personal interpretation, but the outlook of the official leadership of Chabad. I hope, also, that this explication will be valuable for the Chabad movement, which, I believe, is larger than its organization. And I hope that these words will go beyond this audience to reach the much wider community of all those whom the Rebbe touched in one way or another, and will cause something of a shift.

When we speak about the coming of Mashiaḥ, we speak about a mega-event. We may never be fully prepared and we may not know the details of how, what, or when, but we are talking about major changes. One of the consequences of this statement is that, if we are expecting things to change in a major way, we will have to make major changes. And one of these changes is that we have to cast away a huge number of petty quarrels; our insignificant clashes are not only vicious and unprofitable, but ludicrous. Next to the truly momentous changes we are anticipating, all our trivial arguments shrink into trifles; our disputes are comical, not just painful.

I am not speaking only about personal quarrels, but about all the political trappings you deal with in this country, and that we deal with in Israel. Many of the things that people fight about are the sheerest, shallowest nonsense, especially if we compare these quarrels to the establishment of an entirely different order.

In this context, whether Party A or Party B will have a particular right or a particular authority seems ridiculous. Who will remember all the foolish people fighting about such things? When the tidal wave envelops the world, no one will remember if my shop was on the west side of the street or the east side. Everything will be moved.

So the coming of Mashiaḥ means, among other things, the casting away of internal squabbles. We must abandon, for example, the Jewish interdenominational quarrels, many of which are associated with small, short-term calculations. What will be better for my organization, for my little group, for my little cause in the next two, three, or five years? How will I gain a little more support from this rich man or the other rich man? How can I manage to be written up in one newspaper or another? Compared to the big things, it's all foolishness, all vanity.

It is important to talk about the future, about what people are going to do when the time comes…and the time is coming, whether we want it or not. We must talk to people about what Mashiaḥ means. The status quo will change, and all these petty issues will be swept away. There are so many things we must do.

So what do we do?

Let me start by saying something about Israel. We are stuck in a very unfortunate position. We try to move to the right, and the way is blocked. We try to move to the left, and the way is blocked. We try to go forward, but we cannot. We try to retreat, but we are cut off. So, we are surrounded and blocked on every side.

There is one direction, however, that is not closed: upward. That route is still open, and we should try to move in that direction. We should do it not just as a statement, as a slogan, but as a serious practical move toward a different way of life.

This does not mean we should cast away all kinds of things we are dealing with and start dealing directly with the divine. It does not mean we should forget to eat our breakfast (people won't forget that even in the World to Come). But we can put our lives with their little crises in perspective, and when we put them in perspective, they will become very different, because our real concern should be with the Above.

In a more concrete way, it means being genuinely concerned about every segment of society, not just in working on the details, but in major areas: addressing the rifts among ethnic groups and the growing gap between rich and poor; making education (not just knowledge) a primary and universal ambition, and bringing the whole country – not just a segment of it – to an awareness of the divine.

It also means being careful not to use the Almighty to achieve narrow benefits (even praiseworthy ones), but to remember that all of us, right and left, are the people of God.

This is the direction for the Lubavitcher movement, our orders, if the movement is to continue and progress. So much has been done; so much has been achieved. In some places, the achievements are marvelous, unimaginable. In some places, it is like seeing the flowering of the desert, where Jewish life seemed to be dead, and it has been revived.

But all that is not enough, not nearly enough, because we are now talking about a much bigger process. We cannot stand still and gloat. It is true that when one Jew puts on a pair of tefillin once in his lifetime, there is a new light in the world. It is true that when a Jew does not eat shrimp, even though he still eats other non-kosher things, this is a gain, an advance. Now we have to talk to people not only about small changes, but about major changes, about complete transformation.

We have to face them. They have to see themselves as Jews.

It is not easy to make such changes; it is sometimes difficult to even suggest them, but now is the time to do it. We don't know when, in two years or ten years, but something great is happening. And if we are to be prepared, then we have to tell people to throw away all the nonsense, to stop indulging in things that are not important, to start moving in a different direction. This involves both those who dedicate their lives to this work and those who are volunteers. It means speaking to those who are here and to many more who are not.

We have to start talking now about changing, not just about turning, but about returning on a big scale. "On a big scale" means that it is not sufficient to make token gestures, for example: to say to an older man, "Do me a favor and send your grandchild to study in ḥeder for two hours." Rather, this is about reaching people in a deeper way, getting them to change their lives, to set their priorities where they should be set, and to put their efforts where they should be put, because a time is coming when these are the things that will count.

It will be a different reality. We have to tell people about it. We have to stress it again and again.

This does not mean that we must invalidate what we are doing. We must just work on a much grander scale. We have to act in a much more urgent way. These ideas have to be expressed not only to individuals, but also to organizations, to groups, to the Jewish community at large. We have to repeat the call of the Former Rebbe: *teshuva* now; redemption now. Whatever has been done is not enough. It is never enough. We have to do ten times as much if we want to be ready for the times that are coming.

There is something else we must say, something that has to do with our attitude about the world. The Rebbe began, but we have to continue to say it, not only to our Jewish brothers and sisters, but to all of humanity. We have to talk about the Seven Noahide Commandments, the seven laws that the Almighty gave Noah after the Flood. These commandments are for every human being. We should speak about these commandments not just to individuals, as if we were selling merchandise, but to all the peoples and nations of the world, so that we can change the world.

Our goal is not to pay a compliment to the Rebbe. A new and different world will come in a short time, and we have to address it. We have to tell people that a different time is coming, a time when different things will count. We must get everyone to keep the basic Noahide laws, the laws of nature and the laws of God, and we must bring people together. This is what we have to tell individuals and nations.

How can we do it? We can do it because, in a sense, the Rebbe is behind us, doing and saying these things. It means recognizing that now is the time to go to others and to ourselves, to pay attention to the big things, the important things, and let the small details go.

Our sages tell us, in reading Genesis 49:33, that our father Jacob did not die. The idea is that, as long as there are Jews in the world, the seed of Jacob is alive, and so Jacob lives within us. In everything we do in our lives, a small part of him lives within us. We say in our prayers "David, King of Israel, is alive and enduring," which means the kingship of David never died. Someone could kill the last Jewish king, but no one can destroy the kingship of the Jewish people. It is still alive. We may be downtrodden, we may be kicked, but the kingship of Israel continues.

In that sense, I would say that the Rebbe implanted his spirit in so many people that his dreams, his visions, his insight, and his tremendous desire continue. It was his utmost desire to bring about that big change. If we make that desire our own, then we can say the Rebbe is not dead. The Rebbe is here, when we are here doing all the things that he left in his marching orders. He said we should advance. He said we should not walk, that we should run. We should attack. He said we should go further.

We should do it, and we will do it.

The Library of Congress, Washington, DC
11 Nisan 5762 (2002)

In the Land of Israel

Chapter Seven

"Is Ephraim a Dear Son to Me?"

At the conclusion of the *haftara* on the second day of Rosh HaShana, we read the verse, "Is Ephraim a dear son to Me? Is he a darling child? For whenever I speak of him, I remember him still; therefore My inward parts are moved for him, I will surely have compassion on him, says the Lord" (Jeremiah 31:19).

This verse, in itself, is moving, and it is twice as moving since it is read on a special day, at a special time, in an atmosphere in which the heart is more open.

Who is Ephraim? He is not just one of the tribes of Israel, but a symbol of the Kingdom of Israel, which may, perhaps, be called the State of Israel of those days.

This was an interesting and curious State. It was much larger than the State of Judea, and at times it was even a significant military and political force. Its borders, at its most glorious, were "from the entering of Hamat to the sea of the Plain" (II Kings 14:25). Today, that would be from the city of Horns in northern Syria to the Dead Sea.

At the same time, it was a state with a deeply corrupt political system. This was its basic political pattern: the ruling king would be assassinated by a general, who would then ascend the throne. He would rule in whatever way he would, and leave behind an heir who was, most often, a good-for-nothing who would be deposed by the next general.

This is the succinct political history of the then State of Israel – a state based on a lack of political legitimacy, with all which that entails.

Political corruption, however, was not only internal; it existed also in the international arena. The ancient State of Israel tried to place itself between the two superpowers of the day, and attempted to cheat both, just as it tried to deceive all the other countries with which it had contacts.

And there was corruption in the social and personal spheres as well: in all areas related to money, women, and so on.

Many very harsh things are said in the Bible about this State and its inhabitants. Let me give one example from the words of a prophet who lived in the kingdom of Israel during its most glorious period. Even if one does not understand every word, the verses speak for themselves.

> "When I would [come to] heal Israel, then the iniquity of Ephraim was discovered, and the wickedness of Samaria; for they act treacherously, thieves break in, and bands of robbers raid outside. And they consider not in their hearts that I remember all their wickedness; now their own misdeeds are all around them, they are before My face. They around them, they are before My face. They make the king glad with their wickedness, and the princes with their lies. They are all adulterers, as an oven heated by the baker, who desists from stoking only from the kneading of the dough to its leavening. On the day of our king, the princes became sick with the heat of wine; he stretches out his hand to scorners. For they have made ready their hearts like an oven while they lie in wait through the night; the baker sleeps; in the morning, it flares up like a blazing fire. They are all hot as an oven and devour their judges, all their kings are fallen, there is none among them that calls to Me. Ephraim has mixed himself among the nations, Ephraim is a cake not turned. Strangers have devoured his strength, and he knows it not; gray hair is sprinkled over him, yet he knows not." (Hosea 7:1–10)

The State of Israel of those times was by no means a secular state; such a term did not even exist then. In its own way, it was a religious state, even a Jewish state; not precisely an Orthodox one, but certainly a Jewish state.

True, they did have the golden calves (1 Kings 12:25–33); but they were "ours;" they were Jewish golden calves. Surely, idolatries were also imported from Sidon and Egypt, but the home idols of that State of Israel were Jewish ones.

This religion – which, incidentally, is reminiscent of many modern Jewish movements – was created not out of an inner religious awakening, but out of a strong political desire to detach the States of Israel and Judea from each other.

Thus, a new religion was created that was a Jewish religion, and those who lived by it felt themselves to be Jewish. They worshipped some idols, but kept Shabbat. They committed all kinds of transgressions, but were quite meticulous about the observance of many other commandments. All in all, one can say that this state was not only a traditional one, but one with a clear Jewish character, and a Jewish self-definition.

Opposite the State of Israel was the State of Judea, whose borders nearly reached the Benei Berak of those times. It existed in the part of the land that belonged to the tribe of Dan, and included Jerusalem. This state was what may be termed "the state of the religious."

But the State of Judea was also corrupt, its inhabitants not much better than their brethren in Israel. For instance, the King of Judea brought some idols from Assyria, and the Chief Rabbi of Judea – sorry, the High Priest – put them in the Holy Temple in Jerusalem (11 Kings, ch. 16).

Formally, the inhabitants of Judea went not to the golden calves, but to the Temple; yet the things that the prophets had to say about them were not much better than what they had to say about the citizens of Israel.

Between these two states, Israel and Judea, there were many feuds. Sometimes they only amounted to mutual stone-throwing across the borders, as described in Kings and Chronicles, but there were also veritable outbursts of aggression, and even wars. In one famous conflict, the Kingdom of Israel conquered Jerusalem and broke down the city walls. In another, it won a decisive battle and took a huge number of captives. Nevertheless, Israel eventually gave all the Judean prisoners-of-war shoes and clothing, and sent them home (11 Chronicles, ch. 28).

Why? Because after all, even though these Jews were from Judea and those Jews were from Israel, even though they may have had all sorts of accounts to settle with each other, they still had a feeling of partnership. Therefore even the wars between them could only reach a certain limit, and go no further.

Nevertheless, Israel decided, very clearly and deliberately, to detach itself from the State of Judea and from Jerusalem. It created its own altar – one can almost say, its own deity – and built its own temples, halls, and palaces.

This rift was not merely political. What started out as a temporary political separation became, with time, more permanent, and more internalized. In one cryptic verse, there is an expression which is at least as relevant today as it was when it was first uttered: "Be still, for we may not make mention of the name of the Lord" (Amos 6:10).

The book of Chronicles relates something that happened after the political collapse of the ancient State of Israel. There were still people living there, but they were broken, helpless and hopeless. King Hezekiah, the ruler of Judea, who was a great king, remained the only Jewish sovereign, and he decided to act:

> "And Hezekiah sent to all Israel and Judea, and wrote letters also to Ephraim and Menasseh, that they should come to the House of the Lord at Jerusalem, to keep the Passover unto the Lord God of Israel." (II Chronicles 30:1)

In other words, he sent emissaries to Israel, calling to them: Return home, the Temple is open before you. Please come.

And what was the reaction?

> "So the messengers passed from city to city through the country of Ephraim and Menasseh, even unto Zebulun; but they laughed them to scorn, and mocked them." (II Chronicles 30:10)

So this, too, is not a new thing: King Hezekiah's messengers arrive, and the remnants of Israel, from the tribes of Ephraim, Menashe, Zebulun, and all the other tribes, say (to put it in modern slang): "They want me to come to their Temple in Jerusalem?! Do they think I'm out of my mind? What am I, a *frummie*?" – and they did not come.

All this happened in the distant past. I could have spoken at great length about what is happening now. I am not trying to idealize life here in the recent past. I was born in this country, in this city, and it is indeed a country whose stones are of iron, whose people are of brass (see Deuteronomy 8:9): a difficult land, sometimes even "a land that devours its inhabitants" (Numbers 13:32). This state also has a lot of hard-heartedness, and even a lot of cruelty.

But in the past few years, a relatively new phenomenon has arisen: the legitimacy of hatred. Mutual hatred among Jews is no longer a thing that one is ashamed to express publicly. On the contrary, it has become almost fashionable. It cuts through all sectors – a simple, all-inclusive, fundamental hatred, a hatred that does not even need self-justification. It does not need to say, "I am better, and therefore the others are worse." Rather, it is a hatred based on the others being, by definition, bad. There is no longer a need to call each other bad names; one's very label is enough of an insult: "settler," "ḥaredi," "leftist" – are there dirtier words than these? So the words themselves become foul, and the people become defiled and loathsome in one another's eyes.

It is this that I am trying to fight; surely not on my own, but also not with much company. Sometimes it feels as if I am standing in front of gigantic waves of history that are coming to separate, to cut off, to sever all ties – ties of blood, ties of history, ties of family, ties of memory – and create separate units. And not even units that exist next to one another without touching, but units that operate against each other, nourished by this mutual hatred.

It is a bitter experience to hear people on all sides say: "What have I to do with them? We have nothing in common; let's eliminate them." Everywhere is fighting, confusion and malady, with the groups all working against each other, trying to obliterate whatever is on the other side, as if they were saying: "They shall die, they shall disappear, they shall get out of our lives."

This is much more than a rift. It is a feeling that the others are expendable, that they can be dumped, that they can be ignored.

Surely, this tragedy has not yet actually happened. From time to time, declarations (both sincere and insincere) are made about the need for unity. Life and emotion, too, create aspects of closeness and togetherness. The wars and hostility that surround us create a ring of blood and fire that welds us together, and that welding becomes more tangible in times of calamity.

And yes, despite all their differences, people still go through certain things together, speak to each other, do business with each other, and even marry each other. But alongside all that, hostility and hatred keep growing, and above all, there is alienation, an increasing tendency to move to separate cities or isolated neighborhoods, and to create ghettos: a *ḥaredi* ghetto, a national-religious ghetto, a Sephardi ghetto, a Russian ghetto, a secular ghetto, a socialist ghetto.

And in each of these ghettos, people live together and support each other, reinforcing their faith and their lifestyles while creating reservoirs of ferment and estrangement from, and hatred toward, everyone else. "They" must not sit with us. "They" must not live with us. "They" are dangerous, ignorant, and corrupt. And "they" the residents of the other ghettos – have only one thing on their mind: how to reduce our area of subsistence, how to conquer us, how to obliterate us. Therefore, let us distance ourselves, let us part ways and ignore each other. For after all, what have we to do with them?

And those who rely on books and writers, seek and find (and sometimes even invent) "proof" that it is right to behave like this, and that the hostility, the hatred, the split are justified.

Now I would like to go back to the words of Jeremiah. Jeremiah spoke after the great Downfall. He went through it all. He knew all there was to know about Israel, and he was not a rabbi, nor a TV reporter; he was a prophet. And with this authority of a prophet, he says very harsh things, chastises people, and makes prophesies. Yet there is one thing that neither he, nor any other prophet, ever does: he does not, for a single moment, give up on the existence of the Jewish people – including those parts of the nation that he opposes, that he preaches to, that he admonishes. He can call them "a band of drunkards, adulterers, and liars" (e.g., Jeremiah 9:1); but he never, never, gives up on them.

In one sense, this is the mystery of prophecy, as well as its message. The prophet knows full well who Ephraim is. He knows everything that is written in Ephraim's newspapers, and all about Ephraim's TV shows. He knows what transpires in Ephraim's discos, and he hears Ephraim's dirty jokes. He even knows exactly when and where Ephraim eats shrimp; and he cannot, nor does he have to, say anything good about such things.

But given all that, see how he concludes his speech: "Is Ephraim a dear son to Me? Is he a darling child? For whenever I speak of him," – whatever and wherever he may be – "I remember him still; therefore My inward parts are moved for him, I will surely have compassion on him, says the Lord."

13 October 1997

Chapter Eight
Israel at Fifty

Formally, the modern State of Israel was established in 1948. The process of its creation, however, began a few years earlier. In the distress and struggle that characterized the years before Israel's declaration of independence, the *Yishuv* ("Settlement") that emerged here was both a source of glory and the root of the problem. Not only a new settlement, but also a new kind of Jew was created here, a new species that undoubtedly wanted to be – and in many ways, indeed was – very different from the Diaspora Jew. This new Jew clearly parted with the past, and created new things. Many were extremely beautiful. There were also a number of questionable elements, but at any rate there was something new.

This "New Jew" was no longer the wretch who was beaten up and remained silent; he had learned to fight, to stand on his own, to strike back. He had also ceased to be a creature of the air, the lumpenproletariat of the world. Rather, the New Jew began producing basic products, and made a tremendous effort to return to the soil, to put down root, to cultivate it and be cultivated by it. Indeed, one of the characteristics of Jews living in this land – which may seem immaterial, but which is deeply significant – is that they plant trees. Diaspora Jews, even landowners, do not ordinarily plant trees. This reflects the inner conviction that life anywhere in the Diaspora is temporary; there is always the possibility of having to move – either by choice or by force – to another land, a different exile. Even when people do not think about it consciously, they feel this impermanence. For the Diaspora Jew, "soil" is, at most, what one treads on as one wanders from one place to another. Here in Israel, however, people plant trees not only because they know they will be there to see them grow, but also because they feel that they belong to this place, and that their children and grandchildren will sit in the shade of those trees.

A new language, too, was created here. The revival of Hebrew is a unique phenomenon. In Ireland, for instance, the government is devoting resources to reviving the Gaelic language – used by an ever-decreasing number of people – with no apparent success. Yet Hebrew, which was an unspoken language for so many centuries, has reawakened. To be sure, this new Hebrew is not exactly biblical, mishnaic or talmudic. It is a new type of Hebrew: slightly impudent and slangy, but also full of vitality. It turns out that – both consciously and unconsciously, intentionally and unintentionally – what was severed for two thousand years is now being reconnected.

Let me bring a small example: I was astounded to find very prevalent Israeli Hebrew colloquialisms in the letters of Bar Kokhba.* Bar Kokhba was not intentionally imitated, because people simply did not know about him. It seems that once we returned to the land, we also began, unknowingly, to imbibe from it.

Another significant change in Israeli existence, which has already been pointed out, is symbolized by the word *bitaḥon*.** In the Diaspora, especially in Ashkenazi countries where Hebrew is pronounced with the stress on the penultimate syllable, this word was pronounced *bitoḥen*; here in Israel, the last syllable is stressed, and the word is pronounced *bitaḥon*. This change of stress also reflects a shift of meaning. The exilic *bitoḥen* hinges on hope and faith, while the Israeli *bitaḥon* has to do with power and strength.

---

* Leader of the Great Revolt against the Romans, 132–135 CE.
** Traditionally, the word *bitaḥon* meant "confidence," "trust," "certainty," and "faith." In modern Hebrew, it is mainly used for "defense" and "security."

Such changes were probably inevitable. My parents' generation not only lived in this country; they also laid its foundations, fought for it, and contracted malaria for its sake. And their generation accepted – sometimes with, sometimes without regret – the fact that the generation now growing up would forget some, perhaps more than some, of the sacrifices of the past. Our parents assumed that, in the course of time, we would part with many memories, some of them lofty and glorious. But they also hoped that what would be created here would make the loss worthwhile.

And indeed, along with the *tallit* and *tefillin*, a few other – no less significant elements – have been abandoned. Thus, for instance, Israelis consciously abandoned sophistication and refinement, as well as profundity and intense spiritual activity, for the sake of directness and of being a *Sabra*.

But this was not the only thing that was ceded. For many generations, Jews said in their festival prayers: "You have chosen us from among all the nations; You have loved us and found favor with us and … have given us … in joy and gladness, Your holy festivals." In the course of time, the "You have given us" was discarded, and only "You have chosen us" was left. Here and there, the "You," too, has disappeared, and like a broken record, all that is heard today is "chosen, chosen, chosen."*

Even in Ben Gurion's lifetime, and despite his fervent speeches, we stopped trying, or even wanting, to be "a light unto the nations." Yet who could imagine that we would turn into a little USA so quickly? At one time the Bible – even when it was completely secularized and had become a sort of national deed of land-ownership, or perhaps a socialist manifesto – was a book everybody knew and cited. Today, it is still studied in all Israeli educational institutions – as an extended piece of boredom that no one knows how to get rid of. Once, not so long ago, we were a socialist state – or, rather, a state that stood on the borderline

---

* A similar thing has happened with the hymn of the *Palmaḥ*, the main combat unit of the pre-IDF *Hagana*. The refrain of this hymn said, "We are always ready to [obey] commandments, we, we, the *Palmaḥ*." Although this hymn does not deal with holy matters, it is nevertheless an expression of the willingness to sacrifice and obey orders. Yet here, too, what was left is only the "always we, always we," and sometimes, only the "we, we, we."

between the socialist East and the capitalist West, a state that wavered, and was even sometimes divided, between British orientation and Russian dreams, a state that was proud of its kibbutzim and considered them the ideal. But soon enough we embraced – wholeheartedly – American capitalism, in some of its less attractive forms. Nowadays, the income gap between the highest ten percent and lowest ten percent of Israeli society is the widest in the Western world. In the first years of the Israeli State, we were known as a place where it was forbidden to offer workers tips or bribes. Today, tips and bribes exist here just as they do in much older and wealthier states.

I do not intend to bewail the loss of socialism or income equality; perhaps only to speak a little about fraternity. I marvel at how quickly all these changes have happened. Money is surely an important thing. It has already been noted that money is like a ladder,* because, like a ladder, it can be both ascended and descended. However, when I was a boy, "money" used to be written in lower case. Now it is written with a very, very capital *M*.

Beyond that, it can also be said that in all facets of our existence here, there is an ever-increasing blurring of our selfhood for the sake of imitation. Culturally speaking, we are not even a small USA; we are merely a very provincial province of a great state. We imitate its movies, its way of speech, its slang, its sins – without, however, acquiring its virtues. What is being created here is reminiscent of the description in the book of Nehemiah: a people that, both linguistically and culturally, speaks pidgin English, pidgin Hebrew (See Nehemiah 13:24).

Interestingly, we imitate the US in almost everything except one thing. Here, in Israel, we must "hush, for we may not make mention of the Name of the Lord" (Amos 6:10). Thus, it is strictly forbidden to say "God willing" in military documents. And while the holy Dollar says, "In God we trust," it will be a while before anything like that is printed on the Israeli shekel. And this is just one facet of the terrible, irrational dread that exists here of returning to our roots. I do not know the origins

---

* The numerical value of the Hebrew word *mammon* – money – is equal to that of the word *sulam* – ladder; see Ba'al HaTurim's exegesis on the Torah, Genesis 28:2.

of this terror, for if the *Teshuva* movement is a marginal phenomenon, it will die out; and if it is not – as can be seen in quite a number of places in the East and West – then all the attempts to stop it will be of no avail. However, this fear creates something that is perhaps best described by a paraphrase of a verse in the book of Esther: "And many of the peoples of the land* became *goyish*, for the fear of the Jews fell upon them."** For fear lest, God forbid, someone will become religiously observant, our ignorant Jews are becoming more and more like gentiles.

This horror, which seems to be haunting an entire state, would be funny except for its many sad consequences. One of these is that in our wonderland, whenever a small, temporary partition is erected, it grows into a wall. We sow such small, transient partitions for all sorts of temporary reasons, political or otherwise, or just out of silliness. Yet mighty, almost insurmountable walls spring up.

I am not preaching for religious observance, for such preaching is either unnecessary or ineffective. But all these processes of escape and assimilation have created a distancing from Jewishness. Beyond the relationships among the various sectors of society, abysses of ignorance have been created which are very difficult to bridge. It is relatively easy to be "born again" – yesterday a person was a wicked sinner, and today he is holy. However, no one can be a total ignoramus one day and learned the next. This kind of obstacle is very difficult to overcome.

We thought that the nation created here would be different, that it would not have to be ashamed of its exilic heritage. Yet there is a great deal of atavism. One of Shalom Aleichem's books is a series of letters from Menaḥem Mendel to his wife, Sheina Sheindl, in which he describes his dealings in the stock market of a big city (with the imaginary name of Yehupitz): how stocks gain and lose value, and how he, who does not really understand what is going on, is buying and selling, making a fortune one day and losing it the next; one day he is a millionaire (on paper), on the following day he is a pauper. I remember that

---

*   *Amei ha'aretz*, which in Hebrew also means "ignoramuses."
** Esther 8:17. The original verse reads, "And many of the people of the land became Jews, for the fear of the Jews fell upon them."

when I read this book as a child, I thought it was very amusing, but I was sure that such behavior would never happen here.

I was wrong. Menaḥem Mendel is still alive. Today his name might be Mor or Mohar or Tom or Ben, and his wife is no longer Sheina or Sheindl, but rather Yafit or Grace or Gal; but he is still playing – with or without understanding – in that same stock market.

We have not changed that much, then; we have not really become a different people. All the ancient problems that we had, and that we thought we had gotten rid of – albeit at a heavy cost – have remained. The greed is still here, the selfishness. The desire to be conspicuous and boast exists as always, yet now it is augmented by a great deal of machismo. And on the other hand, a lot of the kindness has vanished, a lot of the enthusiasm has been quenched.

It is both sad and difficult to say this; but now, fifty years after its establishment, it sometimes seems that the State of Israel has rocketed from childhood straight into old age, without ever experiencing maturity. We grew old before we grew up. The young Israeli State is suffering from geriatric ailments.*

Are we becoming a Jewish, more successful version of Liberia? That state – which was established one hundred years before the State of Israel – was also created to bring exiles back to their homeland and give them an independent, English-speaking state with an American constitution. Is this all that the great dream – my parents' dream, the dream of generations – amounts to? Does this justify having lost all that we have lost on the way? What has happened to the dream? "What is come upon us?" (Lamentations 5:1).

Why all this has occurred is a question for historians, but another question is relevant to all of us: Is there a way to change the existing situation, to fulfill the ancient dream?

To answer this question, let's examine the other side of things. We have had an independent state for fifty years; but what is independence? The Hebrew word for "independence," *atzma'ut*, comes from

---

* There is, indeed, such a disease, known as progeria, in which little children – seven-, eight-, twelve-year-olds – suddenly become old and die of old age while still children.

the same root as "self," *etzem*. To be independent, then, is to be more myself. Just as the external, political manifestation of independence is not being subdued by others, so too, the inner meaning of the term is not imitating others. Waving a flag and declaring a government is the easy part; being ourselves is surely a more difficult undertaking.

What is selfhood? How do we become ourselves? In this sphere, various attempts have been made – mostly in the so-called religious sector – to return to the past. However, returning to the past is a dream. It is possible to turn back the hands of a clock, but no one can turn back time. Returning to the past is impossible; it is only possible to be reactionary, which is not quite the same thing. In every way – sociologically and otherwise – being reactionary is a modern phenomenon. It neither stems from the past nor is it connected with it; rather, it is based on the very present present. Attempts to return to the *shtetl* do not recreate the *shtetl*; they create a plastic *shtetl* that never existed. But just as there is no way to return to the past, there is no way to deny it, or erase it. On the other hand, it is possible to build a future; and it is also possible to create a different future, one that will not be a mere continuation of the present.

Seemingly, the best and easiest thing would be to do *teshuva*, let us all be good Jews, just as our forefathers were. But what we really need is to be good Jews in the best way that we can be. A person can be a *tzaddik*, a righteous one – or a *ba'al teshuva*, a penitent. A *ba'al teshuva* can reach a level higher than that of the *tzaddik*, and can be stronger, firmer, more genuine. Yet he is different. I cannot be the way my father, grandfather, or great-grandfather was. Our forefathers were supremely righteous, and they now dwell on high. I have different problems. My problem is not how to be like Rabbi So-and-So: my problem is how, and where, to be my own kind of *tzaddik*, a *tzaddik* in a way that pertains to my own self.

For this, we must draw water "out of the wells of salvation" (Isaiah 12:3), penetrate our own depths, figure out what are mere shells, empty imitations – the desire to get by in this or that society – and to seek out what is real. This is digging for our own soul. Wherever our soul is, it can still hear the echoes of Sinai, and it still says *Shema Yisrael*, even when it is no longer familiar with the verse.

Thirty years ago, I taught a class on the issue of "who is a Jew."

We said then that a real Jew is one who would choose to sanctify God's Name by becoming a martyr rather than worship idols. Jewish history is replete with thousands of simple Jews who died for the sanctification of God's Name. In a sense, the Jewish people is just as proud of its thieves and prostitutes who died in the sanctification of God's Name, as it is of its rabbis and righteous ones. It is the thieves and prostitutes who attest most to the existence of that inner core – independent of tradition or erudition – which is the very essence of a Jew.

One of the students then asked me: This was surely true in the past, but do you think it is still valid?

I did not know what to reply, and the question was left hanging.

The next day, I flew to a kibbutz near Eilat and spoke there. I don't remember exactly what I said, but I do remember that I managed to make my listeners furious. At some point one man got up and screamed: "I am a secular Jew, and so were my father and grandfather; but I am telling you, if someone tried to force me to worship idols, I would rather die."

This was almost like a voice from heaven: I had received the answer some twenty-four hours after having been asked the question, and not from someone who had heard the question, but rather from someone who, in a moment of rage, answered exactly the question I had been asked.

So the essential core does exist, but we have to dig it out. We need to draw sustenance from there – not in order to add more *Yiddishkeit*, not in order to give the Almighty more gains. Had God wanted Torah study alone, He would have created more billions of angels that would study Torah for Him. Had He wanted more prayers, He could have easily made more thousands of legions of praying angels. But for some peculiar reason, He wants us – with our problems and complications, with our crooked, stubborn, tortuous souls. And He has given us the ability to attain independence – to reconnect with ourselves for the sake of our Jewish independence – so that our existence will be based not on "safe borders" or a "safe peace," but on a genuine foundation.

This is what I would really like to wish the State of Israel in its fiftieth year: that it will attain independence. Thus far, we have only had an imitation of external forms: a flag, an army, ambassadors, prime ministers of one kind or another. We have lost some of our selfhood on the way, without obtaining anything in its stead. Perhaps now, in the fifti-eth year, we should re-declare the establishment of a Jewish State; not necessarily with different borders or a different population, but with real independence.

13 October 1998

Chapter Nine

Peace and the Greater Land of Israel

F rom any halakhic discussion of problems relating to the integrity of the land of Israel, many different approaches emerge, and not all of them are compatible with each other. Even a relatively well-defined area such as the halakha is not entirely definite; many things depend on the analysis of facts, on the frame of mind of the decisor, and on the amount of information available to him. Halakha is extremely honest, and often also neutral; yet even though it does not take into account what the world, with its wise men, scientists, and politicians, says, it is not entirely esoteric.

I will therefore touch on some of the problems related to this issue.

The first and most fundamental point is our right to be here. What Israel's Proclamation of Independence says has nothing at all to do with the issue. Our right to this land does not stem from the fact that we have been living here, that we made the desert flourish, or that we conquered it with our army. Jews have been living in various countries for much longer periods than they have been living in the land of Israel.

If time spent in a country were the only criterion, then we would have much more right to Iraq than to the land of Israel!

Our most fundamental claim, the one over which there can be no argument, is the right of the promise which the Almighty made to Abraham and his descendants in the Torah: that this land is ours. Of course, whoever does not believe in the Giver of the Torah and in the Torah has difficulty speaking about "the right of the Promise." Nonetheless, this is indeed our only real claim, the only true charter we have. And if we are here by virtue of the divine Promise, our presence has moved into a sphere that is not affected by *realpolitik*.

A part of the divine Promise specifies the borders of this Land. We who believe in the Promise also believe that eventually this whole area will be ours – whether in ways that we can plan, or in ways that will be totally unplanned. The problem facing us today is not whether or not the Jewish people has an inherited right to Israel, but how this right can be realized within the existing situation.

It is well known that to conquer the land of Israel is a commandment. However, from the halakhic point of view, it is not clear whether this is a Torah-based or a rabbinic injunction, and where and how it is to be applied. At any rate, it is clear that the halakha does not consider the conquest a positive commandment binding on every Jew at every time and place.

Another fundamental commandment is the commandment to settle the land of Israel. This is a very great and important commandment, and one of our major duties.

The question arises, however – how much should we "pay" for the fulfillment of a commandment? What are the most basic commandments, the commandments that must not be transgressed no matter what, and before which every other consideration must be put aside? Now, although there are many commandments in the Torah, and although we are called upon to do whatever we can to fulfill each and every one of them, there are only three about which it says that one must fulfill them or be killed. Neither the commandment to conquer the land of Israel nor the commandment to settle the land are among them.

Another question is this: Fulfilling the Messianic requirements and reaching the full "borders of the Promise" is indeed a mission given to the Jewish people. But is it necessarily binding on the State of Israel? Are the modern State of Israel, its current government, and the Jewish people as it is, currently trying to build its life in this land, the bearers of this mission? Are they the ones on whom it is incumbent to extend the borders "from the entering of Hamat to the sea of the plain" (II Kings 14:25)?

For our people has chosen – temporarily, I hope, and out of recklessness – to try to be like the other nations of the world. As long as we are arguing about whether and how we are Jewish, and what our definition of Jewishness is, then any claim that we have a right to this land because of the divine Promise must be questioned. What is at the basis of our claim – is it a religious reawakening, or a mindless parroting of the mantra "You have chosen us," and nothing more? For being chosen is not a status that stands alone; rather, it appears in the context of "You have sanctified us with Your commandments and brought us close to Your worship." It is much more a matter of duties than of privileges.

If all that we take from this is the "right" to take and to conquer, then we enter the realm called in Jewish sources, "the hiding of the (divine) Face" – or, in other words, we descend into the mire of geopolitics and world history. And if we are a nation like all others, then the laws that apply to them will also apply to us. These laws will banish us from this land, because we are here like a thorn in the flesh, and because we are wicked imperialists, and every freedom-lover has the full right to drive us away and expect universal sympathy. For today we do not justify the ancient threefold connection between the Jewish People, the land of Israel, and the God of Israel.

Another halakhic issue is the explicit prohibition to give a place in the land of Israel to strangers; in the land of Israel, strangers are, at best, tolerated. On the other hand, the Bible itself tells us how one of Israel's greatest kings – Solomon – gave Hiram, King of Tyre, twenty cities in the land of Israel in return for the latter's economic support (I Kings 9).

Neither of the above is necessarily an example to follow, but it shows that things are not as clear as one might think.

From all the above we can see that what we have here is not a political calculation as to how much we must pay for the conquest and settling of the land of Israel, but rather a halakhic negotiation that takes other considerations into account. One of these considerations is the value of each individual life. As we know, according to Judaism, the worth of every individual is immeasurable; saving a life (*pikuah nefesh*) overrides everything else. Yet *pikuah nefesh* is not only the saving of a single life in the present, but also the saving of many lives in the present and the future.

Had there been a possibility of reaching real peace in return for territorial concessions, I think that, halakhically speaking, it would have been permissible to make territorial concessions. Not everyone who believes in the Torah and wishes to fulfill the commandments is a political hawk, thirsty for war and unwilling to make sacrifices. However, at this point in time the question should not be asked, since in the current situation there is no room to talk about peace.

There have been many wars throughout history, and some have lasted over a hundred years. Yet none of those wars ever had as its sole goal the entire uprooting of a certain state and a certain people. The Arab world, on the other hand, does not accept our being here *in principle*. It is in no way ready to have us live in this place, and has no intention of getting used to our being here – and I don't think it is only the wicked rulers who think so. The Arabs' intention is to wipe us out completely, Amalek-wise. At most they are willing, in return for concessions, to make some statements and sign some documents that would hardly be worth the paper they are written on. Any armistice, on Arab terms, only gives them the ability to rest in order to attack us again and destroy us more completely. And let me add one more point: The world will not be sorry if we are lost; on the contrary, it might be quite happy if the savage Arabs did its dirty work.

To sum up: In the existing situation the question of peace vs. the integrity of the land of Israel is moot, since there is no basis and no room for talking about making peace. It is not the halakha that is the obstacle: it is reality that binds us to fulfill the commandment of *lo tehonem* (Deuteronomy 7:2) (which, according to our sages, means, inter alia, not to give strangers anything in return for nothing).

If at any point in the future the Arabs come to accept our existence, then such talk may be considered. But then again, I think that once the Arabs agree to our being here, they will also be willing to give us land even "from the river of Egypt to the great river, the river Euphrates" (Genesis 15:18).

9 April 1970

Chapter Ten

Unity

Many aspects of life in the State of Israel are not in our hands. We argue, rave, and fight about economics, foreign policy and related issues; but in truth, most of these are controlled by outside forces. We can affect them only minimally. Still, there are some areas even – if they seem more restricted – in which we have significant influence, and on which we can have considerable impact. These include social and educational issues, the responsibility for which is, to a great extent, ours.

One of these issues is Unity. Everyone, both in and outside of Israel, writes and speaks about the differences and rifts in Israeli society. I sometimes think that all those involved in the different organizations and institutions working for unity could themselves make a sizeable crowd. But although those who strive for unity are so many, their actual influence is small. One reason for this is because they don't seem able to unite with each other. Perhaps this is because in most cases the desire for unity is defined as follows: Everyone knows I am right; once everyone else accepts my views, the Jewish people will be unified.

Since it is this kind of unity that most individuals and groups speak about, it can be easily understood why unity does not blossom from among them.

This is one problem.

In addition, some of the issues about which we argue are indeed serious, so it would be wrong to say that none of the differences of opinion are important. We fight over questions such as what the borders of the land of Israel should be, the ideal character of the State of Israel, what the Sabbath and Yom Kippur should be like. It is precisely because these matters are significant that there are disagreements about them. Questions such as will Mr. So-and-So be appointed to this or that position, these are unimportant. But questions such as what kind of life we are going to lead here – in Jerusalem or in Tel Aviv, in Kiryat Shemona or in Migdal HaEmek – are real problems which are not amenable to simple solutions. Much of the talk about "loving our fellow Jews" and about bringing all Jews together may also be attempts to plaster things over, to paint everything in monochrome, and to behave as if no differences exist. Yet differences do exist, and they are not only real and painful, but also likely to remain with us for a while.

(Needless to say, I always take into account the possible arrival of Mashiah, when all our problems will be solved. Incidentally, I believe that both the Jewish people and the entire world are much more ready now to receive the Mashiah than ever before, which is a significant improvement. Yet when we speak not about the eventual coming of the Mashiah, but rather about our present problems, we are speaking about a culture war. Nor is it one single war, but rather a number of wars taking place simultaneously – over culture, policy, and social structures. Some of these wars are very quiet, but they do exist and go on.)

But as long as we are speaking about different camps – even about rival ones that literally throw stones at each other – we are speaking of normal national existence. Jews have always lived with controversies. Psychologically and sociologically speaking – and this also has a sound theological basis – Jews behave as a family, and in a family, siblings always fight with and beat each other, often till they bleed. Does this mean they cease to be siblings? Not at all; such fights are part and parcel of the family entity. Families survive because of the overriding closeness among their members. Because family members are so close to, as well as in such close proximity with, each other, they often fight. Thus differences of opinion are not a theoretical matter, but rather lead to discord and even violence. All the world's creatures wage their fiercest wars against members of their own kind. It is so with ants, cats, wolves, even moose.

Is this an idyllic picture? Possibly not. But even the prophet Isaiah, who promised that "the wolf shall dwell with the lamb" (11:6), never promised that two lambs will be able to coexist peacefully.

Yet however unpleasant or even dangerous this may be, it is still within the norm. Quite often, though, our internal fighting slides toward a point which I find both dangerous and frightening. I am not making this up. I have seen such statements in newspapers, and even heard them from individuals – not all extremists – from all walks of Jewish society. Everyone – those with the earlocks and those who go bare-headed – speaks in exactly the same manner about the "others." They say, "What have I got to do with them? We have nothing in common." I have heard people make statements such as: "Nothing in the world ties me to those religious people; I feel much closer to the Arabs" – along with parallel statements from the other side: "Those secularists, they are just like the gentiles." Similarly, "settlers" and "left-wingers" may consider each other total strangers.

Such statements express a kind of acceptance, but a very threatening one. It is the same kind of acceptance that comes after the death of an enemy; I cease to fight because there is no one to fight with anymore. The other party has changed to such an extent that it has become a stranger.

This seeing of the other, not as an enemy, an opponent to be fought, but rather as a stranger, seems to me the greatest, most terrible threat to our existence. So long as I assume that I am right and the other party is wrong, we still belong to the same body. I can say that so-and-so is a wicked person and an unbeliever, and should be put to death by one of the four forms of capital punishment (which, according to Jewish law, are: stoning, burning, beheading, and strangulation) – and still feel that my "non-believer" is closer to me than a righteous gentile (*Gittin* 57a). But losing the feeling that we are one, that we are one body, is graver than any controversy, graver even than civil war.

A simile can help us understand this. Diseases of the autoimmune system have become more widespread nowadays. They include diseases such as AIDS, multiple sclerosis, and others, that are not inherently related to each other, except in defining the source of the problem:

a war that the body is waging against itself. One's body cells begin to treat parts of one's body as foreign invaders. The body usually knows itself; one part may be wounded, but the body continues to identify with the part causing it pain. With autoimmune diseases, however, the "I" becomes partial, stilted, reduced, and then some cells begin to do to others what they would do to any foreign body: they try to eject them.

These horrible diseases are not caused by a germ or virus. They originate within the body itself. As in the case of AIDS, the apparatus that triggers this response can be created spontaneously, or due to external stimuli such as foreign blood, or sexual relations with people with whom we should not have such relations. But at any rate, the reaction is similar: the body ceases to recognize itself as a single unit, and begins to perceive parts of itself as foreign.

Such a situation is not merely frightening: *it is an encounter with death itself.* As long as every Jew acknowledges that a Jew is a Jew – however much he may fight with him or be willing to cast him into hell – the relationship remains intimate and personal. It is like the attitude that exists within a family. I can be angry with my delinquent brother; I can even throw him into jail, but still, I know he is "my bone and my flesh" (Genesis 29:14), even if we argue, even if we tear each other's hair out. So long as he remains a part of my "I" – the "I" of the individual or family – we can both exist. But the disease currently threatening the Jewish people, in which the "I" ceases to recognize itself as a single unit, a comprehensive whole, this is a state beyond repair. Such a situation is not just a fragmentation, it is not just pain: it is death.

The feeling of "I" is natural. Every baby begins, at a very early stage in life, to coordinate the various parts of its body – even when it is not yet sure what should be done with each limb. When a baby is born, it possibly knows nothing, but unconsciously feels that there is one "I," however dim and vague, from the tips of its toes to the top of its head. This "I" includes all kinds of limbs and parts, some beautiful and some foul. These parts fulfill various functions, some that I am interested in and some that I am not. Yet it is all "I." So long as this unified perception is there, there is existence; once it falls apart, existence ceases.

When we examine the referent – the state of the Jewish nation – we see that this simile has both theoretical and practical implications. I am not talking about creating unity. Unity is a grandiose thing, a supreme cause, and, God willing, the time will come in which we shall attain it. I am talking about something more urgent, more essential: pulling out of the syndrome of this incurable disease, in which I cease to feel that my "I" includes the other. I may have a very negative view of Reform, Conservative, and Reconstructionist Jews, but all of them are "I." I may argue with all those people whom the late Prof. Leibowitz termed "desecrators of the Sabbath, who have sexual intercourse with ritually impure women, and eat non-kosher food," but they are still "I."

So long as this collective "I" exists, we have life. It is this all-inclusive "I" of the Jewish people – not a unified Jewish people, but a people with an "I" that includes all its members – that we must not lose.

October 1999

Chapter Eleven

Prophecy and Government

There is a political system that has never actually existed. It is an ideal – although only partially idealized – system: that of the ancient Jewish State. The prophet Isaiah says: "The Lord is our Judge, the Lord is our Lawgiver, the Lord is our King; He will save us" (33:22). This statement, which anticipates Montesquieu in describing the three arms of government, expresses a very clear and radical position. It says that the sole source of political and judicial power or legitimacy is God; He is the Lawgiver, He is the King, He is the Judge.

Politically, historically, and theologically speaking, God ceded two of His functions to man. He gave kingship – the administrative arm of government – to the king or other authorities. And to the judges, He gave judicial power. He did not, however, cede His power as Lawgiver; all laws are God-given.

Consequently, in Jewish law there is no constitutional body that can create laws. The Torah laws are treated not as arrangements for social order, but more like laws of nature. Like the laws of nature, they can be explained, explored, even manipulated, but never created.

As for the other two arms of government, the book of Judges tells of judges who were in many ways like rulers arising from among the people, without any apparent government structure. They served as both judges and kings. Later on, with the anointing of kings, the two arms were separated.

Without a legislative counterweight, the judges were given almost boundless power, possibly unparalleled in any other system of government. Judges were not appointed by the administrative arm, whereas the Supreme Court, the Great Sanhedrin, had the power to interpret the Law – no small matter, even in countries where the judicial arm is restricted.

Indeed, one of the problems in Jewish law – which also exists in modern times – was how to control the judges. In times past, control was exercised in two ways. First, the *Sanhedrin*, consisting of seventy-one people, was a large enough body that impetuous decisions were unlikely. Secondly, there were very high demands made on those seventy-one members in terms of knowledge, and even more so in terms of personal integrity. The members of the *Sanhedrin* had to be not only above suspicion, but almost more than human. A judge who had any kind of a personal blemish was immediately, and permanently, disqualified.

Once kingship was instituted, and there were two arms of government, the possibility of clashes arose. For example, in Jewish law, there are two kinds of wars: aggressive and defensive. A Jewish ruler can declare a defensive war without consulting anyone, but is not permitted to declare an aggressive war without the consent of the *Sanhedrin*. (Similar distinctions exist in American law.) But who decides what is an aggressive war and what is a defensive war?

The definition is often in the hands of the newspapermen in the countries involved.

Within the Jewish system, there is no constitutional way to resolve clashes between these two arms of government. However, there is an element that seems to have no parallel in any other system, and which is both political and a-political. I am referring here to the prophet – not as an individual with a religious or moral message, but as a political institution.

According to Jewish law, a prophet can veto, or initiate, practically anything, in any sphere: military, religious, judicial, and administrative. Interestingly, it is the judicial arm that decides who is a true prophet; a false claimant is liable to the death penalty. But once a person is declared a true prophet, he can have tremendous power – provided he is obeyed (which was not always the case). At least twice, the Bible relates how a king declared war, possibly a justified one, and the army was ready for battle, but a prophet came with a divine message not to go to war, and so there was no war.

One such case – somewhat reminiscent of the history of the United States – happened in the days of King Rehav'am, son of King Solomon (I Kings 11–12). Some of the Tribes of Israel had decided that they did not want to continue living under the old kingdom, and went on to form a kingdom on their own. King Rehav'am, who was the suzerain, and theoretically the only legitimate king, declared war, and was about to invade the territories – which in this case were in the northern part of the country – in order to impose unity by force. But a prophet came, saying: "God says there should be no war," and so the army went home. As a result, for several hundred years there were two separate kingdoms. In other cases, prophets insisted on going to war, or taking other steps which seemed politically unwise.

In addition to making or breaking wars, a prophet can suspend any law, but only temporarily. A prophet who tries to interfere with the basic system of law, saying: "God says such-and-such a law should be changed, or interpreted differently," can be condemned to death. He may, however, say that for a limited period – a day, a year – Shabbat will not be observed, or Yom Kippur will not be celebrated.

Politically speaking, the institution most similar to that of the prophet is that of the Roman dictator. Dictators were given supreme yet temporary power, in order to cut across the lines of regular government; so long as they reigned, the government was suspended. Similarly, the prophet operated only in ad hoc situations, and his position was entirely temporary. Yet, unlike the dictator, prophets could only be acknowledged, never declared or appointed, and their appearance on the historical stage was sporadic and unexpected.

For a system which had ceased to function properly – due to corruption, size, weakness, or any other reason – a prophet thus represented an external power that could open new vistas and make decisions. By temporarily suspending laws that had seemed unbreakable, the prophet was able to restore a system's ability to move and to change – something which could never have happened otherwise.

In fact, impasses can hobble practically any system. Moreover, it has been mathematically proven that no system can solve its problems from within itself; an outside power is needed.

What would be the nature of such a power in political life?

From the dawn of history, countries have generally behaved immorally. Machiavelli did not invent Machiavellian tactics. He probably just described what he saw at the Borgia palace. An old definition, which I think is quite true, says a diplomat is "an honest person sent to lie for his government." Interestingly, diplomats may consider their job painful, but never shameful. Is there any kind of supreme morality that operates even in politics? Is there, can there be, "kosher politics"?

A case in point is the Nuremberg Trials. These trials were basically anti-democratic, and not only because the conqueror enforced its notion of what is just on the vanquished. That is a small thing, done quite often over the centuries. The Nuremberg Trials attested to the notion that there is a supreme Law, able to override even the will of the people (which in so many places is the main source of legitimacy). For remember, the Nazi regime and its laws were created democratically, and were therefore "legal." In other words, there is "legal" and there is "right."

In this sense, the Nuremberg Trials were influenced – perhaps unknowingly – by an entirely different concept of justice. In other words: there was a clash between the decisions of a democratically elected government and the commandment "Thou shalt not kill," which may also be described as a prophetic statement.

If we accept that such a statement has more authority than human systems of government, we also accept that there is indeed something beyond the ordinary sources of legitimacy. Such a law – which may be defined as "natural order, law, and religion" – should have stronger standing in human consciousness than man-made law, and be accepted as the source of all legitimacy. Lincoln expressed this notion via his belief that there are things to which simple people will never agree, that Everyman will not accept.

Can there be such law? If so, what would its source be? These questions were relevant not only for the ideal Jewish state of 3000 BCE, but remain relevant for us today.

Furthermore, in contemporary society, with all the complex situations that are created daily, is any agency deemed capable of intervening to resolve an impasse that threatens to paralyze us? In other words, is there a modern analogue to the role of the prophet? And if so, who can fulfill it? Who will be the modern-day prophet?

As it happens, there are many candidates. For many years, the great hope for humanity was the scientist. Scientists and laymen alike believed that science could provide the remedy for all human folly. Indeed, many scientists took upon themselves the role of high priests, or prophets of a new order.

This notion has collapsed entirely. In fact, scientists today, especially in the spheres of nuclear and biological research, are confronted with grave moral questions. Who decides such things? What is the source for the legitimacy of such decisions? Or, in other words, is there "kosher science?"

Journalists have a role somewhat analogous to that of the prophet. Their influence is so great that many people tend to attribute supernatural powers to them. The first journalist, in this sense, was Socrates. In his "Apology," he compared himself to a pestering fly that makes the body politic move. He was, incidentally, one of the first to interview people, doing so in such a way as to lead them to the solutions he already had in mind for the problems he had raised. Interestingly, Socrates spoke, in this context, about being driven by his "daimon." So what makes the journalist speak? Is it an angel or, as Socrates put it, a devil?

Another aspect of journalism, one that sets the journalist apart from the prophet, is that the journalist is a kind of entertainer. Although he is enormously influential, he is also dependent on his readers, his editors, the owners of his newspaper. The prophet Hosea (9:7) says: "The prophet is a fool, the spiritual man is mad." A prophet can say things that are not only unpopular, but also unthinkable. The media person, on the other hand, cannot afford to sound crazy. He has to convince his readers that he is right, and in this sense, he has even less freedom than the medieval court jester, because he does not have the protection of being able to present himself as a fool.

Additional candidates for the role of prophet were the geniuses –
Nietzsche's Zarathustra, and others – and the artists. As for the Church,
in many countries it does indeed have huge power; yet most religious
leaders lack prophetic abandon. Often, their arguments are just as convincing as that of the Jewish apostate, who converted to Christianity
because he believed that it is better to be a rich professor in the big city
than a poor *melamed* in the *shtetl*. This is a convincing argument indeed,
but what kind of a message is there in it?

Of all the candidates for the role of prophet, then, I do not see
anyone who can truly fulfill it.

A different approach may be found in the Talmud (*Pesaḥim* 66b).
Hillel, one of the greatest sages in Jewish history, was once asked a question, the answer to which he had forgotten. "Said he to [the questioners],
'I have heard this halakha, but have forgotten it. But leave [it] to [the
children of] Israel; if they are not prophets, they are the sons of prophets.'" That is to say, leave the people alone and they will be able to find
the solution themselves. Which is what actually happened.

This anecdote expresses a basic trust – which is perhaps also a
need – that even though people may not be prophets, they are "sons of
prophets." The term "sons of prophets" is found in many places in the
Bible, in the context of "schools of prophets" (groups of disciples who
learned to prophesy). If we concede that existing systems will not always
provide solutions, and that there is an entirely different way, this will
lead many people to try to be prophets. So perhaps prophecy, instead
of being given to this or that individual, will be granted to the group;
perhaps we can have a nation of prophets.

Finally, must this external force, which solves the internal problems of systems, this "natural law," be of divine origin? Or can it also
be based on ideas developed throughout the ages as to what is just and
unjust?

I believe that the divine fills all of existence, and that whatever happens in the world is divine epiphany. As the Midrash puts it
(*Bemidbar Raba*, 12): "There is no place empty, without the *Shekhina*,
the Divine Presence." The Divine Presence is always there; we just have
to discover it.

But we have no machinery for invoking the divine, for bringing it into this world. We are caught in our own systems. How can we transcend these systems? Even if we had more knowledge than we do, we would not be out of the woods; we will eventually come to the limits of our knowledge, and be faced with the unknowable. So we hope that something not yet taken into account will come up: an unexpected event, a new discovery, a crank idea, a lunatic plan – anything that will upset the equilibrium, slash through the knot.

The best way I know for invoking the divine is by prayer. But what is prayer? Once, when my daughter was two and a half, I was home, praying Minḥa (afternoon prayer). It was the first time she had seen me doing so at home. She tried to speak to me, but I did not answer. She was bothered by this, and when I finished, asked me what I was doing. Being a young father, and thinking I was clever, I gave her an answer that I thought was both true and meaningful. I told her I had been talking to God. She then asked me something that I've been thinking about ever since. She asked me: "And what did He answer you?"

I think this is the real question. We may sometimes be able to pose questions to God; but how can we learn to listen for His answer?

In the Middle Ages, they used to say that the highest point of knowledge is to know that we do not know. Yet there is a tremendous difference between the "I don't know" of the ignorant and the "I don't know" of the learned person. The difference is as great as that between the naïveté of a child and that of a person who knows a great deal, yet remains innocent.

We, as human beings, are at the point of sometimes being able to ask questions, or begin a prayer. We believe – as the Ba'al Shem Tov said – that the words of God at Mount Sinai are eternal, in the sense that He is still speaking them.

God is still speaking; it is we who no longer hear. But if, in prayer, we will try long enough to listen, too, we may perhaps get to hear something.

13 November 1990

In Communities,
the World Over

Chapter Twelve

The Time Is Short and the Work Is Great

I am going to say a very personal discourse on the Mishna in Tractate *Avot* (2:15): **"The day is short, the work is great, the laborers are idle, the reward is abundant, and the Master is pressing"** – from both a personal and a general perspective.

I will begin with the personal aspect. **"The day is short"** is a discovery I make daily. I wake up in the morning, and within a very short time I discover that it is midnight or 2:00 a.m. And I wonder: what has happened to that day? Where did it evaporate? Every Rosh HaShana I regret that there is no double leap year, with a second month of Elul. Had there been a second Elul, I might have been able to finish something before Rosh HaShana. But there is no second Elul, and again I feel that I am short of so much time. The day is short, amazingly short, and it ends with tremendous speed, and thus weeks and months and years go by.

"The work is great," too, and for some reason it does not seem to diminish as I keep working at it. And I can attest that the other paragraphs of the Mishna also hold true for me. This is my private view.

But in addition to the subjective "short day" of an individual life, there is also the objective "short day." In the past, this was not so obvious; but now, everyone can see how the day is not only short, but also becoming shorter and shorter. Processes that we assessed would take dozens of years are now unfolding within an exceedingly short time, and the world is trembling and changing speedily.

I would, however, like to focus on our "day," the Jewish day. The world is agitated and changing; but for us as a people, as an entity, it seems that not only the day, but also our entire life is growing shorter and shorter.

I will mention the world's three major Jewish communities. First, the Jewish community in the Western world. Recently published statistics, pointing to the high rate of intermarriage in these communities, have created a shock that was unjustified; the writing has been on the wall for quite a while. What is happening today in the Western world is not as dramatic and catastrophic as the events we underwent a few decades ago. Still, it may be termed a "self-inflicted holocaust."

It seems that the Jewish people has chosen a method somewhat reminiscent of an ancient Roman custom. How did people commit suicide in ancient Rome? They would get into a warm bath and cut their veins; then sit there and bleed quietly, peacefully, to death. This is what is happening to the Jewish constant bleeding, not unceasing.

In the former USSR, on the other hand, there is a Jewish community of an as yet unknown size. This community, forced into ignorance, is only vaguely aware of its Jewish identity and consciousness. The majority have no knowledge of, and hardly any contact with, Judaism. A forceful, wide-ranging effort may change the situation dramatically. Jewish schools of every level, and communal cultural life, may reemerge there.

This part of the Jewish people is undergoing a crucial time of historic decisions. It may assimilate very fast – or be revitalized into a semblance of its former glory. At present it does not yet have a clear path, and therefore also no inertia of direction. In a very few years, things will become set; but now events may still change dramatically.

The third Jewish community is the one living in the State of Israel. People think that Israel's problem is whether or not we will have a Palestinian state here. I think that a much more serious problem is whether or not we will have a Jewish state here – and I am not talking about the security aspect.

I wish to mention something that should be remembered, historically speaking, too. At present, it is rather difficult to have intermarriage in Israel, for the simple reason that there are no available candidates. However, there is a difference between intermarriage and assimilation. Assimilation, unlike intermarriage, does not depend upon the physical presence of strangers. It can happen *in situ*. And we in Israel can undergo the very same processes as the Jewish communities around us. There is nothing here in Israel that in and of itself sustains Jewish existence in a significant and meaningful way. One small example appeared in the daily newspapers last Yom Kippur eve. They dealt with every conceivable subject, but mainly with the war that broke out twenty years ago. None of them, however, mentioned that in addition to the fact that there was a war, this date also happens to be Yom Kippur.

Some two thousand years ago, we were in a very similar situation, whereby almost all of us became "Palestinians." Jews were living in the land of Israel in relative independence, assimilated into the dominant Greek culture. And just as not all the Hellenizers prior to Judah the Maccabee were well versed in Aristotle or read Hesiod, so too the assimilators of today do not all read Shakespeare or listen to Beethoven. Rather, this is assimilation into Michael Jackson and Madonna, as effortless as stopping by the Jerusalem stadium two millennia ago.

The late Israeli President Yitzhak Ben-Zvi said that there is more Jewish blood in the veins of the Palestinian Arabs than in many Jewish communities, and he had a point. For the Jews in the land of Israel disappeared not because they were slaughtered, but because there was internal assimilation.

In other words, assimilation is not necessarily a Diaspora-related phenomenon. It relates, rather, to the frame of reference of the people as a whole, and of every individual. Indeed, one of the most frightening things is that Israel cannot serve as an historic refuge; we cannot tell a Jew in the Diaspora: Come here, and your continuity is ensured.

All these things are happening now in front of our very eyes. As I said, there is nothing dramatic here; but the time in which things may still change is getting shorter and shorter. When a gap of one generation is created, it is so much more difficult to renew the ties. Years ago I traveled regularly to kibbutzim throughout Israel, and I said on occasion: "If you do not change, your sons will not be able to do *teshuva*. They will have to convert." This holds true for all Jewish communities everywhere. We are living in a generation in which the shortness of time can be seen not in the perspective of hundreds of years, but of dozens of years. Perhaps even in one generation, in which the old ties will cease to exist, nostalgia will no longer have any effect, and much will be lost.

This feeling of "the day is short" is what spurs me in whatever I do, and in my attempts to infect others with the feeling of how short time is, and how it is getting shorter and shorter. People criticize me, saying that I am doing too many things. But in fact, I am doing one thing only: I want to be a partner in what it says in one of the prayers: O Guardian of Israel, protect the remnant of Israel…those who proclaim "*Shema Yisrael* – Hear O Israel." I want to ensure that the existence of the Jewish people be a meaningful one, in which *Shema Yisrael* can be said.

This may not be a great dream, but there is enough work here for an entire generation. And I can see not only the agitation and the constant changes in the world in general, and in the Jewish world in particular, but also the lack of awareness of how short time is, and what a great difference the work of a few years can make now.

"**The work is great.**" Great work is involved not only in writing one more Talmud volume. When I deal with the Talmud, or build an educational institution in Jerusalem, or go to Russia for the same purpose, I am doing one and the same thing. I am trying to preserve the chance, the possibility that the "remnant of Israel" not be lost – not only externally, but also internally. And in order that the remnant of Israel not be lost, we must keep the routes open for all the remnants of Israel, so that it will still be possible to communicate, to talk and to understand, and that the words will still reverberate in the listener's heart.

"The day is short and the work is great," because the work is not just writing one more book or commentary, one more item in one's curriculum vitae. The work is immense because one must see the Jewish people in its entirety, not only this or that group within it. The Jewish people still has a large mass with its own power of inertia. To take this mass and create a significant change in it is "a great work," which is not done by an individual, or even by a group of individuals. I know little of what is going on among those Jews who may be termed "outcasts of Israel" (Isaiah 11:12). Yet I think that I am one of the few people still capable of speaking with these "outcasts of Israel" – from Australia to Rio de Janeiro to Jerusalem. For here, too, we have Jews who are just as estranged and just as distant.

The task is tremendous, and **"the laborers are idle."** This is, of course, also a personal confession. I always feel how assaulted I am by idleness, how I am not doing what I should be doing. But beyond that, the book of Proverbs (4:30–31) describes the idle person: "I went by the field of a lazy man, and by the vineyard of a man void of understanding, and lo, it was all grown over with thorns, and nettles had covered it over, and its stone wall was broken down."

The idle man does not necessarily work less than the one who is not lazy. But the idle person sleeps when he should be awake, at the most critical hours of work. To weed a field before the thorns are higher than one's head is relatively easy. Struggling with a field overgrown with brambles is much more difficult, and not always effective. It is easy to put a loose stone back in place in a standing wall. But if one waits until the wall falls down, then rebuilding it is ever so much more difficult.

Indeed, two verses later Proverbs says (4:33): "A little sleep, a little slumber, a little folding of the hands to lie down." The world is full of kind people with good intentions who will, eventually, reach the same conclusions and act accordingly. But "the laborers are idle," they rest at critical moments; and when realizing suddenly what has happened, they feel shocked. Great confusion prevails, people run to and fro, trying to salvage what they can. Such patterns are not new. They have happened in the past.

Laborers who are not idle do not necessarily have to work harder; but they must work at the right time. These are pregnant times throughout the world. Just as in geology, where fault lines mark off huge blocks of earth, so today we stand at the juncture between great blocks of time. Such junctures are places of storms and volcanoes – as well as of formation. In today's reality, small acts can have far-reaching consequences, beyond imagination; whereas efforts that will be made five or ten years hence will be so much less effective than they could be today. This is precisely the meaning of "pregnant times" – anything can be born. And this is just the time when one must not sleep.

"**The reward is abundant.**" I do not know the rewards given in heaven. But whoever succeeds in doing something in these areas knows that even the reward of an individual person is infinite. I have had the privilege a number of times to see how a fleeting, sometimes accidental, meeting with a person creates something like a candle that is lit. This is one of those "matters which are immeasurable" (Mishna, *Pe'ah* 1:1).

In one such instance, I once wrote a little book. One day a man came to me with a story. He had read the book again and again, and as a consequence made a strange decision. His daughter was autistic, and he suddenly realized he had been treating her improperly. He took her from the institution where he had put her and brought her back home, even though it was quite unlikely he would succeed in communicating with her. He claimed that I had taught him what to do. And there he was, with his daughter who was speaking, communicating and functioning, and he had come to thank me. I, of course, had no idea that I did anything. I am telling this story for one purpose only – to show how great the reward is. A person does a small thing, and its fruits, and the fruits of those fruits, are unimaginable.

And, in addition, "**the Master is pressing.**" There is a Master to the house, and He asks questions, and I feel that He is insistent.

At the beginning of the book of Genesis, which is "the book of the generations of Man" (Genesis 5:1) not only historically, but also in the sense of man's essence, there are two questions, both asked by God. The first is directed to Adam: "Where are you?" (Genesis 2:9) This is a basic, universal question that pertains to all human beings at all times: "Where are you? Where are you in the world?" This is a very personal question that every person hears at one point or another, either overtly or secretly, like someone knocking at his heart's door; and often one is constrained to reply, "I heard your voice in the garden and I was afraid, because I was naked, and I hid myself" (ibid., 3:10). Later in the book of Genesis, however, there is a second question: "Where is…your brother?" (ibid., 4:9) – Where is he? Indeed, it is a part of the universal shame when one answers: "Am I my brother's keeper?" (ibid.).

So "the Master of the house presses," and He asks: "Where is your brother?" Where is he? What is he doing? What have you done with him? And I must be responsible; I can never evade the issue by asking, "Am I my brother's keeper?"

I conclude here. I did not want to deliver a sermon that would be written somewhere in heaven. Or in the words of the Kotzker Rebbe: "Other rabbis want to speak so that their words can reach the sky. I want to speak so that my words will reach the stomach" ("*in pupik arein,*" as he said in Yiddish).

I did not want to say sparkling words about Torah and halakha or mysticism, nor about what can be done and what has been done, but only to infect all of you with the feeling that time is so short, and how can anyone be idle, how can anyone say: "I am not trying to do something"?

28 September 1993

Chapter Thirteen

What Will Become of the Jewish People?

A new slogan, a new cry is being heard throughout the Jewish world: Continuity. But what "continuity" really implies is – a fight for survival, for only when you are on the verge of death do you speak about some kind of continuity. To put it in a different way, we are an endangered species, on the verge of disappearing. Hence the cry for continuity.

Although we are struggling to survive, the way we are living shows we are likely to lose this fight. No, it won't happen overnight; there are still too many of us to suddenly disappear, but as a people, we are on the way out.

I know that some people try to change the picture by juggling numbers. You can always say, for example, that intermarriage adds people to the Jewish nation. But all in all, this is just a scam. If someone did such juggling in a financial report, he would land in jail.

We speak about continuity, and about passing on our Judaism to the next generation. But what is this Judaism? In many cases, it is an empty word. It is what we call in mathematics a "zero group," a notion that contains nothing whatsoever.

Imagine that one has a document that can open the gates of heaven. He takes this document and runs with it to the end of the world. When he finds he is unable to reach heaven in his lifetime, he gives the document to his children. And his children go on running with it and keeping it safe, generation after generation.

But with time, the words – with all the beautiful boxes in which the document is safeguarded – are rubbed away. The people who carry the document are no longer able to read it, and the document itself becomes a faded manuscript. Later still, it is reduced to a mere piece of paper, and even this piece of paper starts to rot.

Yet each new generation takes this heritage and tries to pass it on. Eventually, however, the people who carry the empty box that once contained the precious manuscript will discover that they are running very hard and very fast carrying nothing.

And so they will stop running.

In one way or another, this is what is happening to us. The inscription has faded from our lives. Some of us still speak about our "message," but we no longer know what it is. Not only are we ourselves unable to read it; the words have been entirely obliterated. We have only an empty shell, and even this shell is no longer intact.

So we go on, but for how long does it make sense to run with such an empty thing?

That loss of inner sense is the essence of the problem.

A people cannot just "go on." Individuals can struggle for personal survival; but for a people that knows it has lost, a struggle for survival seems silly. Survival for what? If I am going to lose anyway, if I am going to pass away in a generation, or in two generations – there are all kinds of demographic calculations – why make my own children miserable? After all, my grandchildren will inevitably forget all about Judaism anyway.

If you lack not just hope for survival, but hope for something greater in the future, you cannot go on fighting. With only a past and no future, you cannot continue.

People also cannot go on living in the past, even if the past was entirely nice – and ours was not. You see, the *shtetl*, wherever it was, cannot be re-created. There is no need and no use for it.

For many people, the State of Israel is a vicarious answer for unsolved problems. But you cannot go on living vicariously. Just as I cannot eat for someone else, I cannot sleep for someone else, and no one wants me to beget his children for him, I also cannot pray or study for anyone else. Life is something that you have to do on your own.

(Parenthetically, don't depend on the State of Israel to save everything. The State of Israel has its own problems as a center of Jewish existence. It is struggling hard to survive in that sense. It is not able, now, to do much about saving others.)

There are more Jews, of one description or another, living in the United States than anywhere else in the world – about six million people who can claim Jewish ancestors. All in all, they have done quite well for themselves. But what they have not done is to create a common future. How many of these people of Jewish ancestry have Jewish grandchildren, or can be sure that their grandchildren will be Jewish? That is the real question.

Moreover, while some are very successful as individuals – perhaps as successful as Jews have ever been in any time or place – as a community, as a people, they are third-raters or less. One cannot go on living, striving and struggling, fighting and working, with the knowledge that one is destined to be a third-rater forever.

There is something else I would like to address, not in a more optimistic vein, but possibly in a more challenging one.

Jews in the Diaspora have only two choices. They can either give up, close shop, and say "We are defeated," or they can create a new way, a new hope. If people want to go on, if there is a feeling that there is something in it, if the memory of the half-obliterated document still possesses some compelling power, then Jewish life in this country must be rebuilt.

Let me say something full of *ḥutzpa*: there is a need, a use, and even a possibility of making this place something like *galut Bavel*, the ancient Jewish exile in Babylonia. It is possible to create a second center, comparable to, sometimes better than, the main center in Israel. But to accomplish this, one has to do much more than survive. However, if you cannot do it right – if you cannot create something that will be worthwhile spiritually and intellectually – it is not worth doing at all.

Such an effort would require massive change – not just in priorities, but also in the way people want and do things. It means both a different plan and a different way of planning. It means making big changes in what people are interested in, and in what they invest. You see, Jewish education is not just for children, but also for the parents and grandparents of those children, so as to ensure that every grandchild of every Jew remains a Jew.

People also have to make changes in their own lives. You cannot be a perpetual salesman. And you cannot go on as you have, creating a whole culture on the reselling of *shmattes*. You need a new creativity. And a new creativity means far deeper involvement by a much broader base of people. This is what survival really means. It is a recognition that if you cannot become bigger and better tomorrow, it is senseless to exist today.

The re-creation here of a significant Jewish culture – even if it is different from that of Israel – does not involve counting how many doctors, lawyers, and accountants we have. It is not even counting how many rabbis will emerge from America; that is all a small and partial count. Rather, we must ask ourselves, are we contributing to a Jewish heritage in a way that will be remembered ten generations from now? How many people here will feel distinctly and inherently Jewish? And what will their contribution be to the future? This is the true measure.

To do something like this requires an enormous input, far greater than anything done before. Whatever has been done so far was done with a kind of indulgence money. People paid to get rid of the guilt that came from discarding their Jewishness. But if we want to ensure some kind of a future – not just survival, but survival with hope – we must make a much larger investment. I am not speaking only about spending money, but about something even more painful – an investment of life.

There is an expression here: "Put your money where your mouth is." Instead, I would say people have to put their lives, their souls, where their money is. This is much more difficult.

I would like to finish not with a note of prophecy, but with at least a note of hope. There are still enough people here. Many of them, even though very estranged from anything Jewish, are nonetheless good people. We have here, all in all, a fair number of individuals who are first rate. These people can become the foundation for a different, better future.

But we cannot expect this building to construct itself; it has never been so.

There can be hope in our future, a promise, something to reach for. If we want to have such a tomorrow – a real tomorrow, and not just a bleak putting off of death for another half-generation – it will require lots of effort. But although this undertaking is unprecedented, it can be done.

May 1995

Chapter Fourteen

The Challenge of the Community, Large and Small

Some time ago, I visited a community not much bigger than yours: Stockholm, Sweden. The head of that community was then Jan Nisell, elder brother of my associate, Thomas Nisell, who recently passed away as a very young man. I mention him now not only as a remarkable person, but also in order to say something about his collaboration.

I came to Stockholm and made one speech, and another speech, and a third. It turned out that my visit was possibly the most costly they have ever had; it must have cost them some $650,000. For you see, from that time on, the community changed its priorities. With Mr. Nisell's encouragement, it opened a number of institutions, and renovated not only the synagogue building, but its entire conception of what a synagogue is. On the whole, the community has become far more lively.

Now, your community is even smaller than Stockholm, which means that if you want to do something, you will possibly have to spend more. You see, I am not a preacher. I am not making a sermon. I just want to talk about some things I think are important. People here in Durban keep telling me, apologetically, that it's a small community. Indeed, compared to Johannesburg, or even to Cape Town, it is.

But what is the size of a viable Jewish community? In other words: How large should a community be not only to survive, but to be more than merely marginal? The answer is that it depends on the community, not on its size.

Throughout Jewish history, the size of a community has never been the factor that determined whether it was great or unimportant. What mattered was the quality of its people, and the amount of effort they put into their Jewishness. That was the real key that determined whether a community was weak and insignificant, or glorious.

A few more facts: Most South African Jews are descendants of Lithuanian Jews, many of whom came from small townships, *shtetlakh*. Some of them, such as Shevel, or Volozhin, or Shklov, were considered great towns. But these "big towns" would sometimes contain 200 Jewish families – or 300–400 Jewish families, if they were particularly big. That was all. Smaller villages would contain barely a *minyan*, and yet many of them became famous. Indeed, some of these small towns and villages were among the most illustrious Jewish centers in history. In Rashi's Trois there lived only 150 Jewish families; even in the great Cairo of Maimonides there were no more than 5,000 Jews. Further testimony of this kind is found in the book by the famous Jewish traveler, Rabbi Benjamin of Tudella, in which he described the Jewish communities he visited: 100 Jewish families here, 50 Jewish families there.

In addition, East European Jews were very poor, and the Jews of Lithuania were the poorest of all. Lithuania is a rather poor country to this day, and the Jews of old, compelled to live off the national surplus, were really in very bad shape. The standard of living of some of your grandparents or great-grandparents was comparable to that of the blacks in South Africa's townships, perhaps even lower. A Jewish bourgeois was one who could afford white bread for Shabbat. And yet these small towns and villages in Lithuania at the turn of the century saw some of the greatest achievements in Jewish history and culture.

Let me illustrate this with a story I heard from one of my

school teachers, a typical Lithuanian Jew. His hometown, a small *shtetl*, appointed a rabbi and made a contract with him in which it specified all the benefits the rabbi would get. That community, however, was so poor that all it could give the rabbi was a small amount of money, not even enough to even die on; the right to the milk of one goat; the right to sell salt to the township, and perhaps a little more. This was not because they were niggardly, but because they simply could not afford more; even this pittance was stretching their limits.

The people, who knew the rabbi was a great man, felt embarrassed for being such an insignificant place that could offer so little. The rabbi, who knew the community, wanted to comfort them, and said: There are maps of the world. In these maps, a small town is marked by a dot; a bigger town by a small circle around the dot; and very large cities with conspicuous circles. Very small places are not even marked. Paris, London, Moscow, are all big circles on the map; Warsaw and Vilna are smaller circles, and this *shtetl* is not even marked on the map. These are the maps we see, but there is also a map in heaven. And in the heavenly map, the size of a place is decided according to the amount of Torah learning and mitzvot done there. In the heavenly map, said the rabbi, Paris and London may not appear at all, but our little town is marked by a very big circle.

This, then, is the main thing that makes a Jewish community great.

The difference is made not by the number of community members, but by what they contribute to the community. Most of what is done in a community depends on the efforts of individuals. The law that says that what you put in is what you get out, applies also in physics (the second law of thermodynamics), chemistry, metaphysics, philosophy, economics, accounting, and computers. In computers, they have a very succinct, although not very gentle way of putting it: "garbage in, garbage out." If you put nothing in, you cannot expect something to come out. What you put into the community does not depend on the local rabbi; he can do a little coaxing, goading, persuading, yet the real work is done by each and every one of you, each and every community member. And "you" means everybody – those who come to synagogue every day, those who come once a week, those who come three times a year, and those who do not come at all. All these are participants in the community, and the contribution of each one, and all together, makes a difference.

When I was a teacher, I had all kinds of pupils, including those labeled "culturally deprived." I used to tell those students – and sometimes I would have to repeat it every morning – "There is nothing genetically wrong with you; it is not your fault that you are behind. It just means you have to work harder; but you can do it."

The same applies to you. This community can become one of those places that is forgotten even when it still exists; it can also become a Jewish center of some importance. But that depends mostly on your efforts. The more involved you get, the more will come of it.

I understand that this community, like all South African Jewish communities, is growing old. This is a financial, ecological, and demographic problem. But when a community does not have a school, it is as if it were saying: "We have no hope." When a community has only a few children, it is a sign of despair, in spite of what anyone may say. It is easy to make a one-time contribution of 100, 200, or even 10,000 rand. What I am asking is much more than that: I am asking you to give of yourselves to yourselves.

In the past few years, I have been traveling a lot throughout the former Soviet Union. I meet many people. Some have forgotten they are Jews, and some discover it by chance. While you at least have memories of living Jews, some Russian Jews do not have even that. Yet I am telling them exactly the same thing – you can do it. You can do it, if you will it, and if you hope.

I now have a whole movement there in Russia, with a journal and all the rest. It's called "One Step Forward." And this is exactly the message. I cannot ask anyone to do the impossible, but I can tell everyone: Take one step forward. Do today a little more than you did yesterday. When one person moves ahead, it is like one particle moving forward; when an entire community moves ahead, then – as in physics – it creates a wave. And waves can break walls. Waves can both destroy and create.

The future of this community, then, is in your hands. No one is too old, too poor, or too rich to learn. Nobody is in such straits that he cannot be asked to do something, to give something of himself, of herself.

I am calling upon all of you to take a step ahead. Those who are already putting in some effort should do more; those of you who are here but have not yet done anything should begin to do something.

And I am including all those who are not here, for whatever ideological reason – the *frum*, the more *frum*, the progressive – all of you. Every one of you can take one step forward. And this one step can make a tremendous difference. If you promise to give five minutes a day, then you give something that can grow. In these five minutes you can learn something new, or do something good.

There is no excuse for anyone – young or old – to avoid actual commitment, actual learning, actual involvement. The only reason for not participating is being dead. Only the dead are completely free of worldly obligations.

If we do not want this kind of freedom, we must go on doing. Therefore I urge people in their seventies to begin learning the *alef bet*, because this spurs them to learn more, to do something valuable and important.

The real point in building a community is not to make a new building for the synagogue. The point is to fill the synagogue with people, making it come alive. It is not in doing one-time things, but in getting constantly involved, having a part of our hearts tied to it. There are no precise measures for this. I do not tell Mr. So-and-So to put on another pair of tefillin. The one measure that there is, is this: whatever you do, you can do better, and you can do more of it.

Once a community answers this kind of call, all despair disappears, and things begin to look different. Instead of seeing the future in terms of more tombstones in the local cemetery, there begins to be hope, and once there is hope – who knows?

It has happened more than once in the past that a place that was a God-forsaken wilderness, Jewishly speaking, began shining from the inside. Some of the greatest figures in our history came from such places. This little bit of involvement on the part of every individual is like one small candle. One small candle can be insignificant. Three thousand candles, however, are no longer insignificant. They become something that shines far and wide, and this light can brighten a whole country.

One of the greatest scientists of the previous generation, Norbert Weiner – the man who created the science of cybernetics – once said that the biggest secret about the atom bomb was not how it is produced.

The real secret was revealed in 1945, when the first A-bomb exploded, and the secret was – it can be done.

When you know something can be done, it becomes doable; it is merely a matter of how much effort and money you put into it.

What I am telling you, then, is that in a community like yours, or even smaller, this can be done. It can and has been done in Stockholm, and it can be done elsewhere.

If you do it, you'll see.

Durban, South Africa, August 1999

Chapter Fifteen

Where Do Torah and Science Clash?

T he problems of *Torah umadda* (Torah and science) are vast. No single lecture or article can do justice to the subject. I will not try to give solutions to problems that some of the best minds through the ages have thought about. But I will share some of what I know, with the hope that it will make people think.

I will divide my discussion into two parts. One part is the subject matter, Torah and *madda*, that is, Torah and science, secular knowledge, philosophy – the problematic encounter and the antagonism between the two. The second part will deal with what happens to the person who is part of such an encounter.

The encounter – the clash – of Torah and science has been the subject of any number of books. Some try to prove that Torah and *madda* are identical. Some try to prove that Torah and *madda* are opposites and that Torah should be the only guide, ignoring *madda*. A large number claim that Torah should be ignored and that *madda* should take its place.

When people talk about clashes between Torah and the scientific world, or between Torah and the world of secular knowledge in general, the question arises: in which areas does such a clash occur?

Let's take mathematics. Mathematics is clearly the basis of almost all exact sciences, as well as a number of inexact sciences that try to apply mathematical and statistical methods. There can be some discussion as to whether the square root of two presented in the Talmud is an exact solution or an inexact solution; but answers to this have already been proposed by Maimonides and others. All in all, there are very few clashes between Torah and mathematics.

(One may claim that mathematics is not a science, even though the Hebrew University and many other universities put it among the sciences. One could say that as a subject which deals with purely imaginary things, mathematics should be put in the same department as fiction! Mathematics does not deal with anything real; numbers are pure notions. We encounter two apples, but we do not encounter the number two. The entire field of mathematics is something like a fantasy, albeit a very powerful one.)

When dealing with Torah and what I call the "hard sciences" – physics, chemistry, biology – we also have very few conflicts, practically speaking. The real problem arises not in the exact sciences, but rather in two other areas. The first is the extremely dangerous field of popular science. In many ways and in many fields, popular science has created whole universes of misconceptions that are extremely hard to rectify.

A friend of mine (who, incidentally, is a professor of mathematics) told me about a poll of American university professors taken some twenty years ago. One of the questions was: "Do you believe in God? If not, why not?" This poll yielded two very interesting results. Most of the science professors said they were believers. Most professors in the humanities said they were nonbelievers. And the major reason given by the humanities professors for being nonbelievers was that science had proven religious claims to be false!

This striking phenomenon must be attributed to the influence of popular science. Popular science has a huge impact on people because it simplifies things. For example, in Israel the theory of relativity is translated as *Torat hayahasut*, and the theory of Darwin is *Torat Darwin*. Note the shift in meaning. When we call something a theory, we refer to a certain proposition that tries to explain the world without advancing a claim for absolute truth. When one translates "theory" as "Torah," however, one makes a very different assumption. "Torah" means *the* truth, *the* law, *the* rule.

This shift that happens in modern Hebrew occurs more subtly in almost every literature. When one reads a book on popular science, one does not differentiate between theory and assumption, or notice that one assumption has more basis than another, that one is a guess and another, a very wild guess, or that some of the ideas are well worked out and some are still in the process of trying to piece together phenomena, experiments, and other things into some kind of sensible whole, without any real claim for being the truth, the whole truth, and nothing but the truth.

When one writes a popular book, one has no time to present all the nuances of the issues under discussion. Therefore science is presented as a set of absolutes. In fact, for many people, Nature with a capital *N* and Science with a capital *S* take the place of Torah. The scientist, with his white lab coat, replaces the priest with his black frock. Many people who look to science in this way are intelligent in every other aspect, but have a notion that science is the supreme law. The scientist, in one form or another, becomes the high priest of a new religion. This religion has a tremendous advantage. It works. If you want to see that it works, just observe.

Everybody in the world, in order to exist, needs some kind of theology, some generalized set of ideas that will define values and systems. Some of these theologies are pagan. Some are obnoxious, but they are still theologies. The people who write popular science have their own sets of beliefs. When a person takes his scientific knowledge and tries to present it as an expression of his theological beliefs, the result is some kind of a religion rather than a set of objective facts. For example, the German scientist Ernst Haeckel was a biologist and a very successful popular writer. His brand of Darwinism had a great influence on what is taught in every school system. But because of his personal bias, he was partly responsible for spreading a type of Darwinism that formed the basis of the Nazi ideology. Let me explain.

People may not like Darwin. They may not like his ideas; they may disregard anything he wrote, but they must also recognize that there is no Nazi ideology in his writings. Yet when you take one of his phrases and put it in a different light, it becomes an entirely different thing. What does "survival of the fittest" mean? Darwin does not use exactly this expression, but he deals with the notion. It has a rather specific meaning. When it is put in a popular book, however, especially when the author has his own personal bias, a whole ideology emerges that has the advantage or disadvantage of being considered science, i.e., truth. In fact, even in the so-called hard sciences, one can find evidence of the construction of imaginary worlds that are not really in any way scientific, worlds in which science replaces religion and Einstein replaces *Moshe Rabbenu.*

The dangers of popular science reach even into the scientific community. Popular science is not only science for the ignorant non-scientist. Most popular science is also science for the scientist out of his field. When you have, as in our times, an explosion of information, so that a person is no longer able to be "a chemist" or "a physicist," but must content himself with being an expert in a sub-subspecialty within one of those fields, even scientists have to read popular science. There is no other way for intelligent, knowledgeable people to understand the world. Popular science, then, has been a major contributor to the notion that there is a conflict between Torah and *madda.*

Another set of ideas that has had an even greater influence on the popular mind is the so-called soft sciences, sciences that are not entirely experimental or mathematical.

In America everybody speaks "psychologese." I do not think people can fall in love anymore without talking about relevance, relationships, complexes, and so on. People can no longer use the simple words of the heart because they are so obsessed with popular psychology. And so it is, to a lesser degree, with many "soft sciences."

The soft sciences have one thing in common – many of their basic assumptions are truly theological in nature. They do not stem from facts, but rather from a notion about the universe and the relationship between things. Some of the conceptual structures that people build are amazing, but in most cases they have little to do with anything in real life. Freudian psychology, for example, is a wonderful thing. It has all the beauty of Greek mythology. And even though nobody has ever witnessed an actual Oedipus complex – nobody had put it into a lab to see what it looks like or whether it exists at all – everybody knows about it. The same thing goes for much of sociology and anthropology. Many soft sciences are simply ways of viewing the world, subjective belief systems that certain people espouse. Indeed, some of these views are so commonly accepted that nobody wants to question them.

C. N. Parkinson, of the Parkinson Law, wrote about this with regard to education. What happened to the schools, he asked, when plain, good teaching was replaced by the imaginary science of educationalism? If one were to look for hard facts to prove that people educated under the most modern systems, from Spock onward, are in any way better educated, better behaved, or better adjusted, I do not think one would find such data. I do not see any evidence that those children whose parents raised them contrary to all rules of modern psychology and modern "how-to" parenting books suffered as a result. I have seen some of them as adults – my parents, other people's parents – and they seem to be well-adjusted, nice people. On the other hand, I have seen a large number of people who grew up with "the best" of psychological and anthropological strategies and "the best" teaching methods, and not only are they poorly behaved, but they even know *less*. Sometimes with a simple blackboard you can teach more than with a whole roomful of computers.

What I am trying to say is simply that many of these so-called sciences are really no more than theories. They are pictures of existence that people have drawn. I do not quarrel with a theorist's right to build these images. What I am countering is the claim that these pictures indeed reflect real life.

Most of the clashes between Torah and *madda*, existentially speaking, are the result of clashes in values between popular science and the laws of Torah. Even mathematics, for example, can clash with Torah. Regarding the ratio between the diameter of a circle and its circumference, Tractate *Eruvin* says it is 1:3, whereas the currently accepted opinion in mathematics sets the ratio at 1:3.14. This small problem is relatively inconsequential. However, in real life, when one tries to form a relationship or function in modern society, one's religious values constantly clash with concepts of Western culture, of "sciences" that are really only points of view. Herein lies the real conflict.

The clashes between the Western world and religion – Judaism in our particular case – are mostly the results of clashes with those theories to which people assign absolute values.

The "science" of biblical criticism offers a good example. Every assumption of biblical criticism that has come up against some kind of experimental check has been proven wrong. From the very beginning, up to our times, you can see a continuous line of mistakes. For instance, one of the minor results of the discovery of the Dead Sea Scrolls was that a whole set of theories, from dating biblical books to finding the authenticity of what is called the Masoretic text, was instantly eradicated. And yet, in many universities, people are still teaching Bible according to these disproved principles!

The basic practical confrontation between Torah and science occurs when popularized hard sciences make theological claims under the guise of presenting scientific statements. Popular science penetrates everything, not only scientific, pseudoscientific, and semi-scientific books. When one reads science fiction or a novel, one gets a dose of popular science. Even when reading comics, one encounters some form of popular science. Many of the soft sciences contain accepted notions that are extremely difficult to uproot because they are repeated in every newspaper, on the radio, and on television. They become so overwhelming that one never realizes there is a possibility of looking at things differently.

We, as a people, are *ma'aminim benei ma'aminim*. We are a nation of believers. If we ceased to believe in God, then at least we would believe in the *New York Times*. It is so; it is written thus in the Holy Book! We just changed the holy book.

I remember when the holy book of Spock was everywhere – when mothers would cry if their children did not behave in accordance with Spock's descriptions. When teachers tell their students that the truth is so-and-so, their students believe them. They shouldn't, but they do.

Belief is a good quality, but if one decides to be a believer, one should at least try to find a decent religion in which to believe. The religions that are so common all over the world – the religion of psychology, the religion of sociology, and so many others – are not decent religions.

In our society, common knowledge becomes accepted knowledge. A friend of mine told me a story about teaching a class of foreign students at the Hebrew University. Among them were several Jewish students who had come from Poland in the 1950s. She was teaching a rudimentary course about Judaism and mentioned that the practice of human sacrifice never existed in Judaism. One of the students, a Jewish girl from Poland, stood up and said: "But please, isn't there a Jewish sect that takes blood for baking matza?"

This student didn't invent this notion. Where she came from, it was common knowledge that everybody accepted as fact. She knew that her parents, not being religious Jews, did not practice this custom, but she was sure that most Jews did.

This is the case with many of our commonly held assumptions. They are based on a structure of belief, sometimes of prejudices, and must be encountered as such.

A few weeks ago, I received some Christian propaganda in the mail. Someone had seen my name in a newspaper and was trying to "show me the light." He began with an assumption that he never thought would be doubted: If he quotes something from the New Testament, I have to accept it. It did not occur to him that there might be somebody who does not accept the New Testament's validity.

Torah umadda is, in many ways, a clash between different religions. American secular culture has become a religion, what I call the Hollywood religion. There are also other religions, smaller ones, such as the religion of science and the religion of mystical notions, all of which come into conflict with the true religion of Torah.

In most cases, the conflicts that arise from the daily encounters people have between Torah and science are based on misunderstandings. Often it is a mistake about Torah, and people end up trying to defend the sheer nonsense that they, for some strange reason, believe is *Yiddishkeit*. These people find they cannot continue with their religion because they think it is ridiculous. In fact, their "religion" is indeed ridiculous. When I was a young man, I met someone in Israel who was then a very important political personality (interestingly, he was the son of a famous rabbi, a member of the *Mo'etzet Gedolei HaTorah* in Poland). We were talking, and he asked me, "Where does God put His legs?" For a moment I thought he was joking, but he wasn't. When I tried to tell him that, as far as I knew, God has no legs, he told me I did not know what I was talking about, because his father truly believed that God has legs! I tried to remonstrate. I opened the Siddur and showed him that not only do we not believe that, but we should not: it is forbidden. He ended the conversation by telling me that he was very friendly with the *rosh yeshiva* of Mir, and that he would warn him that there was a person in Jerusalem who should be destroyed.

In a certain way, this conversation is typical of the *Torah umadda* clashes that many people experience. Often they have an encounter, not only of bad science with Torah, but of bad science with bad Torah. That becomes a much more dangerous encounter, because a person may try to defend something that is entirely untrue. With regard to Torah concepts, many people have never progressed beyond kindergarten, and their theological concepts remain on this elementary, even infantile level. It is therefore no wonder that some people spend years creating and defending imaginary points of belief against imaginary attacks by science. In many cases, a whole generation is still defending positions that were espoused by apologetic writers a century ago. Many words and concepts that have become taboo in religious society have nothing wrong with them except for the fact that fifty or a hundred years ago, people for some reason thought them to be problematic. People see problems because they are defending all kinds of old incorrect positions. These incorrect positions may have been used as points of discussion and dialogue, but they should not be taken as *Torah miSinai*.

Thus, a great part of the clash of *Torah umadda* must be attributed to imagination, ignorance, and an inability to face basic problems. But there are other, possibly deeper problems, not so much in the content of either Torah or *madda*, but in the personality of the person committed to both of them.

In our time, most Jews live an amphibious kind of existence, like frogs, in two different realms – that of the Western world and that of Torah. These two worlds are basically different from one another. These differences are not differences between truth and untruth, or clashes between faith and experience. They are the clashes experienced by people who live in these two realms. To believe in a realm other than Torah is not necessarily the result of a sophisticated exposure to *madda*.

In many cases, and for most people, the novel they read, the film they watch, the radio they hear, are parts of a culture to which they assign a value. I am not a great admirer of American culture, but American culture has one vast advantage: it has a great power of penetration.

Look at our grandparents and great-grandparents. Jews lived in many countries in Eastern Europe for a thousand years, yet many were barely influenced by the surrounding culture. My own grandfather was a merchant. He lived in Poland, but was hardly able to speak more than a few sentences in Polish. Even though he had to deal with Polish peasants all his life, I am sure he did not know anything about their culture. He did not know anything about the church, except that when he passed by one he spat, and, as was the custom, recited the verse, *"shaketz teshaktzenu"* (Deuteronomy 7:26), which most people here do not do anymore. There are very few people in America, on the other hand, whose lives have not been deeply influenced by American culture.

I once defined American culture as a composite of money, fun, and chewing gum. Possibly there are some other ingredients as well. However, whatever the culture's values, it is a culture that penetrates. It is a whole world, a whole universe. As a result, Jews in America committed to Torah are somehow living in two worlds that basically contradict one another. The practical problem for most people in this encounter of *Torah umadda* is not that faith is on one side and knowledge is on the other, but that opposite sets of proofs and beliefs are presented by both sides. The problem arises from being a member of two cultures having contradictory claims and assumptions. The real tension is not a function of the truth of these claims, but rather is a result of the fact that people accept both of them. Frogs do very well with their amphibious life, but human beings are much less adapted to living in two worlds simultaneously. The fact is that people who make a conscious decision to live in these two universes are living in constant self-contradiction. I am not speaking about issues of cosmology or the age of the world, but rather about human relations, about what is and what is not important. These contradictions are the ones that really hurt. People connected with both *Torah umadda* in a conscious, willful fashion are, in a way, condemning themselves to a life of constant contradictions.

I have always been struck by the presence of the American flag in many American synagogues. Although Israelis are chauvinists and Americans are broad-minded, I have never seen an Israeli flag in an Israeli synagogue. Perhaps the Reform in Israel have it, but not the Ortho-dox, not even *Mizrachi* or *Gush Emunim*. The American flag makes a very strong statement. It says: "I belong to this country. Even if I am an Orthodox Jew who studies at Yeshiva University, I am making a state-ment that I want to be in two worlds that clash constantly."

I do not believe that people nowadays can entirely avoid coexist-ing in these two worlds. I don't see any Jewish society that has escaped entirely, or can escape entirely, the influence of the Western world, its culture and its ideology. There is no such Jewish society – not in New York City, Monsey, Monroe, Me'ah She'arim, or in Benei Berak. It does not exist. The infiltration, on different levels and in different ways and forms, is total. It is very hard to build a ghetto wall that will stop culture. A ghetto wall may stop people, but it is not a very good defense against ideas, a way of living, or a way of thinking.

There are people who accept this reality, and say, "We now testify that we are indeed willing frogs." Some people pretend they are not yet on this level, but it is no better than pretense. They are what I call quasi or hidden frogs. For example, I know that there is protection afforded by a black hat, a long coat, beard, and *payos*. But it does not provide real immunity to the influence of a different, contradictory world.

Almost everybody belongs, one way or another, willingly or unwillingly, knowingly or unknowingly (as in the words of *Al Ḥet*), to these two worlds. No one escapes, and the issue of what can be done about this is as real a question as any of the general scientific questions that arise in connection with the *Torah umadda* controversies.

First of all, we must face reality and acknowledge that living in this country (it is true all over the world to different degrees) means being in a difficult position, spiritually and psychologically. It means being under the influence of conflicting powers. To define a problem and know what the problem is about, is itself a great achievement.

Once I see the problem, I have to make decisions on certain issues. What is my primary relationship and what is my secondary one? To whom do I really belong? What is my first world? What is my first country? To what am I really faithful? These are decisions we are forced to make because, in many ways, the problems we encounter repeat themselves as a result of the clash between two different voices that we hear at the same time. The miracle of *zakhor veshamor* is that two different voices came at exactly the same time. Most people suffer from hearing conflicting voices in the decisions they make. Whether it is a big decision about a career or a small decision about something else, there are almost always conflicting notions. There are two ideals, two worlds, two different points of view. Even when I make a choice, the conflict is not resolved immediately, but at least I know where the conflict is.

For example, Jewish society, in its very basic assumptions, is built upon a hierarchy. Communist biologist J. B. S. Haldane described in his book, *The Inequality of Man*, the notion that the inequality of man is still a basic aspect of Judaism. We have different levels for *Kohanim, Levi'im, Yisraelim*, for men and women, for scholars and ignoramuses, and so on. Therefore, if you live in a society that claims that there are no differences, that everything is equal, you have to make a choice between the assumptions of that society and those of Judaism.

Most of the matters that have a great influence in our Western world send one basic message: everything is permitted as long as one doesn't hurt others. The Western world is the universe of consenting adults. However, when one is in a Jewish culture with a Jewish environment, one has a very different point of view, and these two points of view cannot be put together. One cannot make any kind of compromise between them. Both of these worlds as they exist now – the Jewish world and the Western world – have one thing in common: they are internally consistent. At a certain point, however, a choice must be made. Doing so does not mean that life becomes easy, but it becomes something that can be dealt with.

What cannot be dealt with is a contradiction that one does not know exists. When a person thinks, while sitting in silence, that he is listening to what is called "the thin small voice," sometimes what he is really hearing is the radio. The culture in which we live sends all kinds of messages in all kinds of forms, and sometimes it calls for a response. However, if one does not know where these messages are coming from, one becomes confused. If the voices being heard cannot be identified, the response will not always be correct.

Does this mean that we have to go to a desert or an island to cut ourselves off from any communication, or back to the *shtetl* of two hundred years ago? I don't think so. It is enough that we understand that we are not just some kind of amphibious creature, but rather humans living in two worlds. Then we can begin to address the implications. I am not saying that it is easy, but I think it is possible to accept the knowledge and messages of the Western world as challenges that must be met, without always being forced to reject or contradict them. We must accept them into the universe of our existence. Every type of message we receive from the surrounding world has to be checked. Is it a truth or is it a mere assumption? Is it a cultural notion? Is it some different type of notion? So many parts of the messages in this country and many others are, for example, secularized Christian notions. When we encounter them, we may say that we do not accept them. But at the same time, some of them are wonderful. For example, I do not think that there is anything wrong with using radio or television, or any other product of technology, for Jewish purposes. I personally believe that progress is good, and that it goes well with our Jewish notions. I do not think that becoming a reactionary is any kind of answer, that hiding in a hole will provide a solution, because the things that surround me will follow me. What I am saying is that I have to face them. There are certain things I will not accept and certain things I will accept willingly and place within my system. Indeed, not only do I not see anything wrong with them, but I see them as something of a discovery.

Let me conclude with a story: An old rabbi in Jerusalem was in hospital and began to talk with the person in the next bed. This other person was an educated man who wasn't religious. For some reason, the nonreligious man brought up the story of Gilgamesh – the Sumerian story of the Flood – and he was sure that the rabbi would immediately say something against it. To his astonishment, this rabbi, who was just a simple man, was delighted. He said: "You know, my whole life I've wondered: Why doesn't anybody except the Jews remember the Flood? Why isn't it mentioned by anybody else? Now you have answered a question that has bothered me for the past fifty years. Thank you for that."

There is knowledge, there are things to ponder, and there are questions to ask in the encounter between Torah and *madda*. I do not have to accept all of Western culture with everything in it. I have a right, indeed an obligation, to look at it and establish my priorities. What is my basic faith? What are the things I value the most? Yes, I am living in a different culture that, in certain ways, is an antagonistic one, but I still have the ability to make choices, to dissect problems, to deal with each of them separately, and to make decisions.

I have not offered a solution to the problem of *Torah umadda*. I have tried, however, to say something simple: life is a very complex thing. It is not hard to be an angel in heaven. It is not hard to be a beast on earth. What is really hard is to be a human being. We are constantly fighting the battle which in one way can be expressed as *Torah umadda*. In another way, this battle defines our existence between the poles of body and spirit, heaven and earth. All these are different ways of expressing our position and our need to make decisions, to take sides. We know we can never answer our questions by going completely one way or the other, but, hopefully, we can learn to find some practical way to live as human beings in this world.

Torah u-Madda Journal, 1994

To the Individual

Chapter Sixteen

The Golden Mean and the Horses' Path

The Golden Mean, the middle way between extremes, the path between contradictory positions, is the basis of Maimonides' ethical theory. Maimonides speaks of avoiding extremism and choosing the moderate way as the apex of Jewish and human elevation. According to him, any tendency toward the extreme, even if that extreme is usually considered good, is a saddening deviation, whereas the middle path is the good and true way.

In striking contradiction stands Rabbi Menaḥem Mendel of Kotzk. When this rabbi was asked why he was so extreme in his views and conduct, he took the person who asked to his window, which opened to the street, and explained: "You see, the two sides of the road are for human beings; only horses walk in the middle."

The Kotzker Rebbe thus defined the middle way, the average between extremes, as "the horses' path," the way animals walk. Men must choose one extreme or the other; if they fail to do so, they are merely horses.

These two approaches seem to utterly contradict each other,

unbridgeably so. Yet a bridge must be created. Surely we can assume that Judaism has seen differences of opinion in regard to many problems – and especially regarding this issue – in which differences of temperament and character determine one's approach. There is no doubt a fundamental difference between Maimonides, the symbol of stable solidity, and the Kotzker Rebbe, who was so very stormy. But the bridging that must be done is not in order to establish artificial common ground. The fact is that both views are correct, each from its own point of view, and it is therefore incumbent upon us to find a relationship between them, so that we can determine our own stand in this matter.

Objectively and theoretically speaking, the golden mean is surely the true way, the most choice path. In the Bible and in the writings of the sages, this idea is stated often, explicitly and implicitly. In the Kabbala and Hassidic literature, too, the constant opinion is that the middle way is the true way. In fact, many of the underlying assumptions of Hassidism are based on the recognition that the difference between good and evil in general is the difference between *Tikkun* and *Tohu*, the average, sedate order and the unrestrained wildness of any kind of extremism.

But just as the middle way is the line of truth in theory, psychologically speaking the Kotzker Rebbe is correct; for what human being, full of good will and yearning for truth and holiness, can help going to extremes?

True, this extremism may not be according to the pure truth; but can an enthusiastic man, yearning for God, stand between extremes, measure and weigh things so as not to leave, Heaven forbid, the golden mean? Who can, in the midst of ecstasy, check whether or not he has deviated from the middle way – if he is not a horse?

But if we re-examine these two approaches, we shall see that the contradiction is in fact imaginary, for the two positions do not deal with the same issue.

There are two paths, both of which go in the middle, between extremities. The golden mean and the horses' path are not at all identical. The horses' path is the plodding average between extremes, a necessary result of the lack of power and courage to take one of the extreme routes. People who cannot muster the energy to devote themselves totally to something, anything, always walk in the middle, wanting to please everyone, and pleasing no one. Always haunted by alternative motivations, they make silly compromises. They measure the middle path against the standard of their own smallness and try to walk there; but in truth, it is the path of horses.

The golden mean, on the other hand, is more than the simple average between extremes. In fact, the golden mean is the merging of extremes. It is made for people who are full of true passion and great enthusiasm, people who can take two extremes together, and whose souls can thus accommodate the merging of both extremes – the golden mean.

Just as the horses' path evades extremes, the golden mean embraces them within a oneness that unites them. Those who take the golden mean do not measure the middle, because the golden mean can encompass any extreme position, since its adoption is precisely in the adherence to extremism.

The golden mean and the horses' path may seem to run along the same middle line; but the horses' path is beneath contradictions, while the golden mean is above them.

Reshafim, 1958

Chapter Seventeen

Heroism

I would like to start with a thought I brought up last year: the feeling that here, at this time and in this place, we are on a kind of island. All around us the world is boiling, full of trouble, while we are in a sort of bubble.

On one hand, it is pleasant to be in a bubble, but on the other, it is forbidden for us as Jews to reside in such an oasis of calm and quiet, even temporarily. Even when one has glimpsed lofty states of existence, one must remember that the great Ladder that reaches the heavens is firmly grounded in the earth. And the earth is not always a comfortable place, especially in our day, when it is shaking, quivering, and wet with blood.

This is why I choose to speak this time about a less abstract topic – Heroism.

The simple definition of heroism is the one we find, for instance, in the story of Samson: taking apart the gates of a hostile city and carrying them away, grabbing a lion and tearing it in two, toppling a building and killing three thousand people.

But there is also a different definition. In *Pirkei Avot* (Ethics of the Fathers 4:1) it says: "Ben Zoma says … who is a hero? He who conquers his desires. As it is written (Proverbs 16:32): 'He who rules his spirit is greater than he who conquers a city.'"

Ben Zoma was considered the greatest expounder of homilies, so much so that the Mishna (*Berakhot* 9:5) says, "When Ben Zoma died, there were no more expounders."

But where is the novelty in Ben Zoma's words? It seems that what he says is stated explicitly in a Scriptural verse! Is there a need for the greatest of expounders to rephrase a Biblical passage?

Yet what at first glance seems self-evident is not simple at all. For the verse is actually not telling us anything about the essence of a hero. It also does not say that he who is slow to anger, or who rules his spirit, is a hero. It only says that one who is slow to anger and rules his spirit is a better person, in moral and human terms, than one who can "rend a lion as one would rend a kid" (Judges 14:6).

So Ben Zoma's homily is based on a more fundamental awareness. By saying that the person who is slow to anger (who rules his spirit) and the hero (conqueror of cities) are analogous to each other, the verse is actually saying that they belong in the same category. It is impossible to compare two things that have nothing in common. One cannot say, for instance, that an elephant is bigger or smaller than a mathematical equation, because they are not of the same kind. Every comparison is based on the assumption that the things being compared belong to the same set, are on one and the same scale, and can therefore be juxtaposed.

Ben Zoma's innovation, then, was that he saw the verse as telling us that there are different kinds of heroism: the heroism of he who rules his spirit and subdues his evil nature, and the heroism of a person who can "devour the arm and the crown of the head" (Deuteronomy 32:20). And it emerges that one is preferable to the other.

Here in Israel, we have become well acquainted with heroism of the first kind. We have had many soldiers who endangered their lives and displayed bravery in war. But it is the second kind of heroism that I would like to speak about; a more private heroism, the heroism that brings victories within one's own soul.

It is a different kind of heroism not only because it is mostly spiritual, but also because it reveals a different aspect of what it means to be a hero.

We can learn something about this kind of heroism from the second verse of the Shema, which is, perhaps, the second most significant in the entire Torah. This verse (Deuteronomy 6:5) says: "And you shall love the Lord your God with all your heart, and with all your soul, and with all your might."

The classic commentary on this verse is found in the Mishna (*Berakhot* 9:5):

> "With all your heart – with both your impulses [the good inclination and the evil inclination]; with all your soul – even if He takes away your soul; and with all your might – with all your wealth."

According to this interpretation, what seems at first glance to be an ascending order is not; heart, soul, and money!? Although our sages state elsewhere (*Hullin* 91a) that "the righteous are fond of their wealth more than of their own bodies," when most people are faced with the choice of "your life or your money," even the most righteous tend to sacrifice their money.

And even if we interpret "with all your might" differently, as meaning "giving beyond measure," the question remains: in what way does "with all your might" represent an ascending order within that verse?

I have been struggling with this question not as a commentator, but as one who recites the Shema; and here is the solution I have found.

"With all your might" does not mean that a person is commanded, "give your money now!" but rather, "give your money always." To negate wealth as an ongoing, constant way of being means that a person is sentenced – be it by himself, or by others – to a life of hardship. In this sense, "with all your might" implies a giving, not of a person's life, but of his soul – little by little, day by day, year by year, through poverty, affliction, and suffering.

The heroism that expresses itself in sporadic outbursts of bravery, such as jumping into the line of fire to save one's comrades, is momentary; while the heroism implied by "with all your might" continues day after day, year after year, in distress, poverty, and need, even in a state of hopelessness.

Incidentally, throughout Jewish history, this latter kind of heroism has played a much more significant role than that characterized by dying in the sanctification of God's Name, of giving one's soul in the literal, immediate sense.

Whoever defined himself as a Jew seldom had to pay for it with his life. But the practical significance of such a self-definition was that a person sentenced himself to live on the fringes of society, of having to be twice as good as the next person to have a slight chance of reaching similar status, a life in which one works much harder and receives much less. In general, a life of poverty and need.

The devotion and self-sacrifice involved in loving God "with all your might," then, is a continuous kind of devotion – day by day, year by year, without seeing an end to it and without expecting a better and brighter tomorrow.

This worldview exacts a heavy price, not only economically, but also in terms of how one experiences life. My wife once said to me that at any party where there are Israelis and others, she could immediately tell who the Americans and Europeans were – they laugh.

Indeed, at a party in which Israelis participate, it is rare to find people just standing around and laughing. It is not because people here are always sad, but because life here is always enveloped in a feeling of dread, pressure, and heaviness. There may be moments of joy, but "bearing the yoke and keeping silent" (see Lamentations 3:27–28) is the norm.

It seems, however, that this is about to change. Throughout the world, people who once recognized only the heroes of battle are now learning about the need for this other kind of heroism. The world, that has seen and sometimes even admired the heroism of violence, must now learn the kind of heroism that has nothing to do with swords, cannons, and bombs. It is the heroism of the person who lives in an extended state of terror, knowing that his next bus ride might be his last, and that danger lurks everywhere – and yet does not break down, and rules his spirit, and is slow to anger, and keeps going.

This heroism is the ability to endure constant distress and pressure, and still live and build, and continue fighting this war in which there are no immediate prospects of victory. It is the ability to live a life of quiet courage, ongoing self-sacrifice. This kind of heroism lacks the grandeur that is the share of the conqueror of cities; for conquerors of cities are honored with triumphal processions, but nobody throws a party for a person who rules his spirit – especially since tomorrow, and the day after, he will have to do it again and again.

The contemporary hero, then, is not the one described in *Pirkei Avot* (5:20) as being "heroic as a lion." In fact, a lion is a very lazy animal who does absolutely nothing most of the time, but has the ability to summon enormous strength in a second and do something spectacular. The "heroic as a lion" kind of hero has great powers that are neither constant nor stable, but are revealed in one extreme outburst.

The contemporary hero, the one whose heroism is not discernible, is the greater hero. It may be the man who wakes up in the morning and opens his grocery store even though there was a terrorist attack there the day before. It is the person who does not flee into forgetfulness, or to a "safer" place, but rather continues doing all the things that must be done. It is that person who walks with his backpack, and continues walking even when he gets hit; the person who, when his buildings are destroyed, rebuilds them; who, when his plants are uprooted, replants them; who, when his descendants are killed, gives birth to new ones.

Thus, we have the level of loving God "with all your heart." Beyond that, we have "with all your soul," which is the one-time sacrifice. And above and beyond that is loving God "with all your might," which is the determination to continue indefinitely, although the future is unclear and there is no promise as to when the struggle will end.

This heroism is not fit for movies or theater. Neither is it fitting only for the great and powerful. This heroism is also for the simple and the small. It is the heroism of "when I fall, I shall arise" (Micah 7:8), of "a just man falls seven times, and rises up again" (Proverbs 24:16).

The just man falls seven times because he is no angel; he is only a just man. Angels fall only once, if ever. A just man falls and falls and falls again, and there is no guarantee that after the seventh fall his trials and tribulations will end. He may even fall seventy-seven times, but is commanded to "rise up again, rise up again."

This is precisely the kind of heroism we need now: the heroism to continue in a situation where no promises are made, in which we know nothing about what is going to happen. It is the heroism of falling and rising and falling and rising again and again and again. "In quietness and in confidence shall be your strength" (Isaiah 30: 15).

I hope that we shall have the strength for this kind of heroism, so that we can be "as the sun when he goes forth in its might" (Judges 5:31) – able to keep going with unceasing perseverance, constantly emitting light and warmth.

25 October 2001

Chapter Eighteen

Self-Investigation

The police force sometimes investigates the actions of a certain policeman, and sometimes also issues a verdict. The results of such investigations, and the verdicts issued, are usually less severe than if the investigation had been conducted by an external body. The reason is self-evident. When people judge one of their own, they tend to find extenuating circumstances, so that even when the defendant is found guilty, he ends up with a lighter punishment.

One can raise many arguments against such internal investigations, and many of them are fully justified. The investigating body does not necessarily distort the truth deliberately; but it may well be accused of favoritism, of unbalanced or inaccurate appraisal of the situation. Therefore, in every properly functioning body, people try to keep a distance between investigator and investigated, defendant and judge.

There is, however, one major exception, and that is when a person has to clarify and judge his own actions. In such cases, every individual is an entire court; he is the defendant, the witness, the investigator, the prosecutor and the judge, all in one.

Such internal court cases occur every day. Some people may do less of this than others, but practically everyone holds some kind of internal debate about his own deeds. Even when the accusations originate from the outside, it is the person himself that assesses the charges: "They say I did so-and-so. They think I am guilty of this or that bad action. They say I am such-and-such a person. Now I am discussing and judging the matter within myself."

After such an internal debate, one arrives at a verdict, and passes a sentence.

Every society and culture acknowledges this phenomenon. Every person tends to consider himself innocent, but this does not necessarily convince others; on the contrary, it is expected that a person will justify and acquit himself (including his extended self – his family, his people, etc.).

In clashes that involve two or more parties, it is easier to understand why people refuse to admit guilt even when they are clearly guilty. Both parties to a feud not only *claim* to be right, but are totally *confident* that they are. This holds true not only for delicate problems that have no clear solutions, but also for cases in which any outside observer would agree that one side is right and the other is wrong. The side that is wrong may be afraid, or ashamed, or may want to evade punishment.

But even people who are completely honest may not know all the facts. While we may have a good concept of things from our point of view, we may not always know – even for objective reasons – all the facts about the other party.

This is not the case with self-judgment. At first glance, it seems that in self-judgment, one is in the best possible position. Judging another person is necessarily done from the outside, and even when all the facts are clear, it is extremely difficult to clarify the reasons behind them, the chain of events, and all the thoughts and emotions involved. These are things that cannot possibly be known to an outsider, while they are self-evident to the person himself.

And yet such internal courts are rarely unbiased. Furthermore, all the "participants" – the judge, the prosecution, even the witness – invariably see things from the personal point of view, remaining blind to other perspectives.

Let's start with facts. One does not always remember them correctly. One may, intentionally or unintentionally, forget or suppress facts. In addition, one surely does not know, or has only a dim idea, of how one's actions are perceived by others. For instance, one person may hurt another, physically or psychologically, yet be totally unaware of it.

As for the charges, even when one seeks to be just, there is always a great gap between charges to which one is willing to confess, and what one blames others for. Any deed – of omission or commission – can be interpreted in many ways; or, to use legal terminology, one can decide which article of the law to apply to the charge in question.

Thus, for instance, a thief may claim that he intended to merely borrow some items; an embezzler may say he only took a loan; a person who insulted somebody may say he just used rough language, or was simply joking. And so, even if I accept the charge of having told a bad joke at a bad time, I will still tend to see the error as much less severe than it actually was. Therefore, even when one wants to right internal wrongs (if such a thought ever occurs to a person), one nevertheless tends to be lenient with one's self.

In addition, one's reaction to other people's misdeeds is often characterized by strong emotions: shock, astonishment, disgust, and even profound shame. But when the doer is I, the response is quite different.

Firstly, my personal involvement limits and distorts my ability to see properly. Personal deeds, like good paintings, must be inspected from a distance. Secondly, while other people's deeds may arouse disgust, our own hardly ever do. This applies not only to physical actions or overt aspects of one's personality, but also to hidden thoughts and feelings. A person's private devils may torment him, but they are never as revolting or frightening to him as other people's are.

This phenomenon is most evident when it comes to self-judgment. Any judgment is based on (a) seeing facts properly, and (b) weighing the facts and arguments fairly and honestly. As we said, facts or claims, when seen from inside, are by definition distorted, incomplete, and not perceived in their full severity.

But the main weakness of self-judgment is in the judgment itself, namely, in the consideration of the different aspects of the case.

Even in cases where the law is clear and rigid, the role of the judge is to appraise the different aspects of a case and take into account not only the acts, but also, to a certain degree, their consequences. In addition, a judge must consider the temptation or provocation that triggered a certain act. Juxtaposing these things with each other is a major component of the art of judging.

But when judging one's self, a person tends to understand, feel, and enhance the reasons that made him do what he did. At the same time, one cannot possibly take the other side fully into account – due to lack of information, the inability to enter into another person's heart and life, and the natural fact that one always feels less for others than for one's self.

As a result, the primary inclination is to see the ameliorative aspects of the case, the things that made me do what I did. Even when the facts and laws are crystal-clear, the tendency to be lenient persists. In the words of our sages (*Shabbat* 119a): "A person never condemns himself."

Surely, in interpersonal feuds, and even more so in cases of self-judgment, one often sees one's own faults very well. But even though it is possible to see the negative sides of one's own actions, there is still a gap between what a person considers his own flaw, or irreversible deed, and the actual "objective" judgment of that act. Even when a person does blame himself, and even when that person is otherwise balanced and reasonable, when the time comes to issue a verdict, he will somehow manage to acquit himself.

Causes and effects, dangers and temptations, look very different when seen from within. The most obvious cause-and-effect relationship may seem far-fetched, while unlikely possibilities and improbable conditions somehow look like certainty, or near-certainty. An empty threat may be deemed life-threatening, a very unlikely positive consequence of a deed may be deemed certain, and people find themselves resorting to explanations and reasoning that, if presented by someone else, would have seemed weak or even silly.

And so, even when one has no choice but to consider himself guilty, the verdict will always be the softer "guilty, but…"

This universal phenomenon makes one wonder. What is the point in cheating myself? A wise man once said: "Who can be fooled? God cannot be fooled, because He knows everything. Others cannot be fooled, because they won't let you fool them. Therefore you can only fool yourself. But what is the big deal about fooling a fool?"

Still, people tend to cheat themselves much more severely, and much more often, than they cheat others. Thus, both people who are unwilling and uninterested in seeing the inner truth, and those who are seemingly willing to make that effort, are equally liable to find themselves entangled in a maze of self-deception.

A major reason for this is the problem of criteria. Considerations and judgments are reached through a set of criteria – be they external-objective criteria, or internal-subjective ones. When the measurer and the thing being measured are two distinct entities, we have a system comprising the significant and the insignificant, arguments that hold water and arguments that don't.

But in cases of self-judgment, one is both the measurer and the measured; the scale and the weight placed on it are one and the same. A famous mathematical principle applies here: Any figure can be juxtaposed with any other figure and found to be bigger or smaller; but when we divide a figure by itself, the result is always the same: one. Therefore, when the measurer and the measured are one, the final conclusion, after all the barren reasoning is set aside – the sum total – is always the same: one.

Self-appraisal and self-judgment, then, are flawed not because people are willfully trying to cheat or mislead themselves, but because the measuring instruments themselves are essentially flawed.

It must, however, be noted that sometimes – although rarely – we may also see people who judge themselves with much greater severity than they would have been judged by anyone else. Sometimes a person will never forgive himself for things that he would long ago have forgiven in others.

(A parallel phenomenon, not very prevalent nowadays, is that of internal judgment systems that have a set of laws and considerations much stricter than any external system. Some knighthood orders, for instance, treated their own members with greater strictness than they would treat others – so much so that people who broke the "constitution" of that order had to kill themselves. At any rate, we can see that this approach, too, does not necessarily yield justice.)

Sometimes this may have an external manifestation only, such as a wise man, who is strict with himself but lenient with others, or a person who, when in doubt, will give away some of his property so as not to deprive others of their property.

Both extremes, however, stem from the same place – the feeling (not always manifested externally) of inner glory. Because one thinks so highly of one's self, one judges oneself with greater severity. Things that such a person would tend to overlook in "lesser" beings he will neither forget nor forgive in himself. Some people apply a set of criteria to themselves that is so far above and beyond what they apply to others, and take it to such extremes, that they sink into melancholy, depression and self-effacement.

Here, too, justice is impaired. Just as people so often acquit themselves and see only how pure and flawless they are, so too a person who always sees his weaknesses, shortcomings, sins and crimes does himself an injustice. When a simple Jew, for instance, measures himself according to the stature of a *tzaddik* or genius, he is using a measuring rod that is not suitable for him. Similarly, a *tzaddik* who measures himself against an angel will necessarily be found imperfect – not because he is so, but because he too is using an inappropriate standard.

Human beings have two eyes, not because two eyes necessarily see better than one, but because each sees from a slightly different angle. Only thus is it possible to perceive distances and sizes. Self-examination is like seeing with only one eye; it doesn't really matter whether one looks at oneself from the ground up, seeing oneself as greater than one actually is, or from the top downward, seeing oneself as smaller than one actually is; in either case, the view is distorted. Only the Supreme Judge, the Judge of the entire universe, is "the God of knowledge, and by Him actions are weighed" (1 Samuel 2:3). He can see everything from above, from below and from within, so only He can be a "sole judge" (*Avot* 4:8), while human beings – whoever they may be – cannot. A human can see things from only one viewpoint: his own.

Therefore, in matters of the soul one should consult with others; not necessarily because the other person is wiser or more understanding, but simply because he has a different way of looking at things, and therefore his reasoning may be more balanced, more just.

This is why our sages say that even the wisest of men needs an advisor – because seeing things from another angle gives the picture depth. Even if one does not have an authoritative figure with whom to consult, one can seek out a close friend with whom he can share his deepest thoughts and feelings, and thus come as close as humanly possible to a just verdict.

September 1991

Chapter Nineteen

Gemilut Ḥasadim

The idea that professionals should deal with community needs is a very modern one. In olden times, all community affairs were taken care of by laymen – often, the best people in the community. They did this work "for the sake of heaven," because everyone believed it was important, and that such work shouldn't be done in return for any kind of honor or remuneration.

There is a story in the Talmud that expresses this (*Horayot* 10a–b): A certain leader in *Eretz Yisrael* wanted to appoint two other sages to public posts. They refused, saying it is not proper to be rulers over others. He replied: "You think I'm giving you authority? It's servitude I'm giving you!"

Indeed, many rabbis used to sign their letters: "I am So-and-So, the servant of God's servants in this community."

The Torah commands us to give tithes (ten percent of agricultural produce) to the poor twice every seven years (in the third and sixth year of every seven-year cycle). Nowadays, many people give ten percent of all their earnings to *tzedaka* – a common practice that according to many opinions is a binding law. In addition, every landowner had to give the poor another sixtieth of his produce (corn, grapes, and olives) in the framework of the commandment of *leket, shikheḥa,* and *pe'ah.* In fact, the *leket* (single stalks of corn left behind, and single, or small bunches of fruit left on the vine or olive tree), *shikheḥa* (single sheaves forgotten in the field), and *pe'ah* (a part of the field assigned to the poor) did not belong to the landowner; they were the property of the poor. The land-owner only had the right to choose which poor he wanted to give it to.

Moreover, eating a product that has not been tithed is compa-rable to eating pork. It turns out, then, that one cannot eat before giving the poor their share. In other words, I must give because I want to live.

The underlying idea is that giving to the poor, or helping the needy, is not something that the poor and needy need so much as something that must be done by those who have. Helping others is not seen as a social measure to prevent disasters in the community, but as an obliga-tion imposed on each and every individual. The poor have the right to demand and receive. The giver, on the other hand, does not give because he is kind-hearted, or because he's under some kind of public pressure, but because it is his duty. A person must first give, and only then search for needy people to give to.

Tithes, then, were a sort of tax for the sake of the needy. In fact, as we shall see later, they served as the basis for all public property.

Our sages (*Avot* 1:2) explain that Jewish life consists of three parts: "*Torah, Avoda,* and *Gemilut Ḥasadim.*" *Torah* is the five books of Moses; *Avoda* is the Temple ritual; and *Gemilut Ḥasadim* is a term that has no adequate translation; even the word *ḥesed* is difficult to translate. *Gemilut Ḥasadim* is, in a way, giving – or paying back – mercy and kind-ness. It is the loftiest kind of giving.

The sages say (*Shabbat* 127b) that most of the good deeds a person does in this world do not carry any kind of worldly reward. There are a few exceptions, however, as it says in the Mishna (*Pe'ah* 1:1): "These are the things the fruits of which a man enjoys in this world, while the principal remains for him in the World to Come: the honoring of one's father and mother, deeds of *Gemilut Ḥasadim* … making peace between a man and his fellow, and the study of Torah is equal to them all."

Why is charity not even listed here? Because charity involves only money, while *Gemilut Ḥasadim* is much more than that. Our sages (*Sukka* 49b) list three ways in which *Gemilut Ḥasadim* is superior to *tzedaka*: "Charity is done only with one's money, but *Gemilut Ḥasadim* can be done with one's person and one's money; charity is given only to the poor, *Gemilut Ḥasadim* involves both the rich and the poor; charity is given only to the living, *Gemilut Ḥasadim* can be done with both the living and the dead."

Who is to be considered "poor"? Jewish law (*Shulḥan Arukh, Yoreh De'ah* 253) lists some parameters that make one eligible for "gifts to the poor." But beyond that, there is another legal obligation – to give to the poor whatever that particular person needs. Since every person's needs are different, the community must find out what the needs of each individual poor person are and try to meet them. For many people have needs beyond food and shelter which, if not met, cause as much suffering as hunger or cold. For instance, there are people who would rather be hungry than dishonored.

Two stories from the Talmud (*Ketubot* 67b) illustrate this point:

1) **Mar Ukva** (an exilarch who was also a great Torah scholar):
In Mar Ukva's neighborhood there lived a poor man to whom Mar Ukva was accustomed to send a charitable gift of 400 zuzim every year on the eve of Yom Kippur. One year, Mar Ukva sent the money by way of his son. The son came back to his father and said to him: "The man to whom you send 400 zuzim every year does not need to be given money from charity." Mar Ukva asked his son:

"What did you see that led you to this conclusion?" His son answered: "I saw that they were sprinkling old wine on the floor so that the room would be filled with its fragrance. Surely, if he can afford such extravagances, he does not need to receive charity." After considering the matter, Mar Ukva said: "If this man is so fastidious, he needs to be given an even larger gift of charity." And he doubled the poor man's grant.

11) **Hillel the Elder:**
A story is told about Hillel the Elder that he bought a certain poor man from a respectable family a horse to ride on and a servant to run before him. It once happened that Hillel could not find a

servant to run before the poor man, so Hillel himself ran before him a distance of three miles, so that the poor man should not feel he was in need.

Maimonides (*Mishneh Torah*, Hil. Aniyim 10:7–14) deals in great detail with what he terms the eight levels of *tzedaka*. The lowest level is to give a poor person, directly and ungraciously, an amount of money smaller than he needs. A higher degree is when you add a smile to that small sum. An even higher degree is when the giver knows to whom the money goes, but the receiver does not know where the money came from. And the highest degree is helping another make a living through some sort of partnership.

I once was the middleman in such a case. I met a certain scientist who had a habit of getting into ventures that cost him money, and consequently he was quite poor. This man had a rich brother who wanted to help him. He took every possible precaution to ensure that his brother would not find out. And indeed, the brother, to this day, is sure he is being rightfully paid for his work.

In addition to a detailed discussion of the various aspects of helping others, our sources offer basic ideas as to how this should be organized. Many of the institutions that are commonly considered the fruits of our modern understanding of social needs – e.g., free schooling, free hostels, special funds for special cases or for communal projects, and the like – were created some two thousand years ago.

Furthermore, there are many rulings as to who should be considered for the role of *gabbai tzedaka*, charity treasurer (e.g., *Bava Batra* 8b–9a; Maimonides, *Mishneh Torah*, Hil. Aniyim, ch. 9; *Shulḥan Arukh*, *Yoreh De'ah* 257). The post was one that only the leaders of the community were permitted to fulfill, and there were specific safeguards to ensure that public money was not wasted. One of these safeguards was that money matters were never entrusted to only one person; there were always at least two people who would attend to such things.

A striking example (*Tosefta, Shekalim* 2:1): The Temple contained, among other things, the main treasury of the Jewish people, with contributions coming from all over the world. Those funds provided for the construction of the entire city of Jerusalem and the maintenance of the whole Jewish army. The treasury doors had a lock that could only be opened with seven different keys. These were distributed to seven different people, who had to be present together. There were also complex rulings to make sure that money was always given for the right purposes, and at the right time and place.

The idea behind this is that *tzedaka* collectors should be righteous not only before God, but also in the eyes of men. In other words, everything connected with *tzedaka* must be done in such a way that it can be checked and inspected in every detail.

Public positions, then, were not merely honorary. It may even be said that the opposite is true, for whoever holds any kind of public office is bound to be hated. The Midrash (*Shemot Raba* 7) says that when Moses appointed Joshua as his successor, he warned him that people would be bad to him, curse and hate him – yet he must love them and be good and nice to them.

Leadership is no bed of roses; yet it must be undertaken lovingly and without remorse. Furthermore, one should assume leadership positions not out of a craving for honor or power, nor because one cannot bear to see other people suffering, but because it is the personal obligation of every Jew to do something for his fellows. Consequently, every Jewish community had numerous "societies" – learning societies, *Tehillim* societies, societies for helping the sick, for marrying off the poor, for helping poor parents after a baby's birth, and for almost any other conceivable purpose. And of course there was the burial society, the Ḥevra Kaddisha (literally, "the holy company"). Since the task of this society was so very unpleasant, it became one of the leading societies in the community, and it was an honor to belong to it.

Finally, it says (*Torah Ohr*, by Rabbi Shneur Zalman of Liadi, page 1b) that a person who fulfills a public role honestly is rewarded in that "his mind and heart become a thousand times more pure." Why? Because working honestly for public causes is extremely difficult, time-consuming, and generally thankless. It means being involved not only with private worries, but also with communal dilemmas. Yet when such a person manages to study for half an hour, he gets much more from it than another person who studies twenty-four hours a day. Because of this, the devil is afraid of such people, and does everything he can to prevent them from studying for even half an hour.

This gives us some idea of the extent of personal growth and development that comes from dealing with public needs. For one thing, a person who deals with other people's needs tends to forget about his own. But beyond that, real community leaders must grow in every possible way in order to truly appraise the problems they are facing and understand what really must be done. In many Jewish communities, it was customary for such leaders to enroll in learning societies. Sometimes they would actually study there, but at least they were enrolled – not just to teach others, but also for the sake of personal growth.

26 September 1971

Chapter Twenty

One Step Forward

Rabbi Aaron of Karlin – one of the first great Ḥassidic leaders – once set out to influence Rabbi Haike, a righteous and learned man from Amdur, Lithuania, to cease living in seclusion and join the burgeoning Ḥassidic movement in order to influence the society around him.

Rabbi Aaron did not deliver a lengthy sermon. He said a single sentence: "When one does not get better, one gets worse."

These few words were enough to shake Rabbi Haike's soul. Until that moment, he had considered himself a saintly Torah scholar, but this one sentence haunted him. He started thinking: "I may be a fine person, but I am not getting any better!"

Finally, he got up and joined the Ḥassidic movement. When he returned to Amdur, he deeply influenced his townspeople.

Had I had as much power as Rabbi Aaron, I too would have said just that one sentence; but since I do not, I shall have to elaborate on it.

This sentence holds true about everything in the world. Nothing ever remains totally stable. Some things are relatively stable; but generally speaking, there is a dialectic, namely, the more alive a thing is, the less stable it is. Only objects that do not interact with anything else remain stable for relatively long periods. But whatever does interact with its surroundings cannot remain in its current state. This is as true for keeping house as it is to running a state, for the life of the individual, for the history of an entire society, and for the world of flora and fauna. Whenever no additional effort is invested, whenever an attempt is made to keep things in one place, there is decline.

This fact is much more evident, true, and painful in the CIS. True, the very fact that you are reading this article, your very connections with a society that identifies itself as Jewish, and your openness to things Jewish, all constitute a tremendous change compared with the state of things here in the past. But this dramatic, historic change has been mostly on the theoretical level. Practically and objectively, there is still so much to do that one should ask oneself how long one should be content to remain on more or less the same level?

In regard to the state of Jewry in the CIS, such questions must be asked sincerely and courageously.

In every family there is the paradox of the good kid and the bad kid. The good kid is always scolded: Why didn't you do such-and-such? Your grades are not high enough; you went to sleep too late; you did not arrive on time; and so on. The bad kid, on the other hand, is in a much more comfortable position. If one day he does not break a window, he is praised by all: How wonderful of you not to have broken or spoiled anything; thanks for coming home before 3:00 a.m.; how nice of you not to have pulled the cat's tail, etc.

Until now, the Jews of the CIS have been "bad kids," and thus whatever they did was terrific and wonderful. Someone teaches another the alphabet – that's great; one does not harm others – it's outstanding; one who knows that he is Jewish and is not ashamed to say this to two other Jews deserves a few medals.

Until now, we have had plenty of that.

Or, to bring an example that does not contain moral judgment: We don't tell a healthy person, "You look so good, your cheeks have better color, your breathing is fine." Such things are said, rather, to someone lying in hospital barely alive. When a very ill person suddenly moves a toe, or eats two spoons of soup, everybody cheers.

A newly healthy person, on the other hand, receives no compliments for walking on his own; indeed, all sorts of demands are made of him. We tell him: now that you are more or less normal, all those things that a month ago were moving and exciting are no longer important. It is high time for you to do significant things.

For a person accustomed to being spoiled and told only nice things, it is not easy to be told: Now that you are no longer dangerously ill, I can demand things from you. The former state of things was surely more comfortable. Indeed, many people wish to remain cripples, because then, whatever they do is not only correct, but beautiful. Every little thing wins compliments. Once they are on the road to recovery, however, they are told: Get out and work. Do something. Start being useful.

You too, now that you are healthier as individuals and as a community, must start to see your main problem as being not "how much have I done," but "how much more I have to do, what work still awaits me." Much more than the fact that I have crawled a few inches from my hole, what matters now is where I am headed. And surely both the personal development and the work that everyone is required to do as teacher, guide, parent, or leader is tremendous.

We are all working against time, both as a people and as individuals. There are two reasons for this.

The first is the demographic situation of the Jewish people in general, and of the Jews in Russia in particular. This situation is simply catastrophic. Formal data about the CIS indicate that for every ten Jews who pass away, only one Jew is born. In other words: there is no need to send anyone to kill the Jews; we are eliminating ourselves. This phenomenon is partially the result of the fact that the remaining Jewish population is largely comprised of old, single people, and it also has to do with the general atmosphere in Russia. Whenever a child is born, it is as if a statement is made: "I believe in the future!" When people do not believe there is a future, children cease to be born. This is just the simple physical aspect of the issue.

The second reason is the issue of Jewish identity. Most of the people who belong to the Jewish people ethnically – even those whose last name is Shapiro, Rabinowitz, or Zalmanson – belong only ethnically. As living people with a national or individual self-definition, they do not belong. It really does not matter if your grandfather was a rabbi or your great-grandfather was a *tzaddik*.

Someone once called this "the potato culture"; meaning that the best part is buried in the earth, whereas what's above the surface isn't worth much. When the best thing one can say about a nation is that its citizens are like potato leaves, then that nation is not a living thing.

Yet all is not lost, since one can see a broader, clearer picture from the outside. But at any rate, the conclusion is that in a situation like this, whoever is "inside," at the core, must work ten or fifteen times harder in order to achieve something. In plague-stricken places, one who has recovered must take care of an entire city. In a city of the blind, a person with one eye is king.

This is a very heavy responsibility.

In terms of Jewish life, the former Soviet Union is in about the same state as a plague city. If I am the only one who can still see, it means that all the others are my responsibility. So I must do much more work than I would, perhaps, have liked.

Each one of us must therefore take up his obligation, perhaps not well-defined, yet concrete for all that. As a slogan for this movement – and not a slogan of the Comsomol – I would use "One Step Forward."

This does not refer to Supreme Causes or to great needs. Rather, it says that every man, wherever he may be, must take one step forward. To use Mao Tze Tung's aphorism: "Even a journey of a thousand miles begins with a single step."

Yes, each of us is at a different point, both geographically and on the chart of his or her own life. Truly, it doesn't matter exactly where people are in terms of time and achievement, nor is the ratio between what they are capable of doing and what they have actually done all that important. Every person has a different personal graph, a whole different world map. What for one person is the past, for another is a still-distant future.

But one thing that people can do wherever they are and they can do it in a consistent, ongoing, defined and focused way – is to take one step forward. Each person can move just a tiny bit, but still a tiny bit forward. The essence of all movement is that one does not remain in the same place. Whatever does not progress, regresses, and whatever does not ascend, descends. That which does not improve, deteriorates; and that which does not become more alive, becomes more dead.

The decision to make time and move one step forward is not the solution to all problems. It is merely a decision to move one step forward, and to keep moving. Wherever you may be, move just a little bit forward. There are people who will progress by learning a new thing; one who today knows only one letter but next week knows two, has taken one step forward.

This is so much to ask – and yet, so little.

This is, in fact, the only way in which movement can be created. When we analyze the motion of a large wave, we see that it moves because almost every molecule in it takes a minute step forward. In this way, enough movement is created to wash over the world.

The assumption is that every man has not only a body, but also wings. And if we ask what we should aspire to reach with these wings, we may use the Kotzker Rebbe's reply: What is man's purpose in this world? To raise the skies.

Ukraine, 14 March 1997

Chapter Twenty-One

On Character Education

Before the Middle Ages, books were very rare and enormously expensive. The most efficient way of disseminating knowledge was through public lectures. Since printing was invented, and the price of paper plummeted, transmitting information by means of the spoken word has become practically obsolete, although it is still the main method of teaching in our schools and universities. Basically, once children learn to read and write – and now they also become computer experts – they can employ other methods in order to receive information.

But this does not mean that schools should be abolished. Even in the modern age, schools and teachers fill two major roles that no book, audiotape, or videotape can: an academic one and an educational one.

The first role – which I will touch on only briefly – is to teach pupils how to learn, which is very different from transmitting information. A coach who teaches someone to run will not run for him; he will teach him how to do the running. This holds true for every subject. To really teach means to get into the mind of the student, to see why he can't grasp a certain subject, and how the problem can be overcome.

The second role of the school is educational: to help form the student's character. This goes far beyond intellectual pursuit. In most schools, the favorite pupil is a little zombie who just sits there and raises his hand at the proper times. But even students who are bright, capable of dealing with any subject, can turn out to be monsters; highly intellectual monsters, but monsters nonetheless. To be sure, the parents have a fair share in the creation of every monster, both biologically and educationally, but modern parents spend a lot less time with their children and are less inclined to invest in them. The power of the peer group has also declined, and thus the educational role of the school has become more decisive, to the extent that the school becomes a kind of foster parent.

In this context, I would like to look into the beginning of the sixth chapter of *Pirkei Avot*, which is called *kinyan Torah* – "the acquisition of Torah."

This text, part of what is known as "Wisdom Literature," is classical, and thus deceptively simple; the reader must work to understand and appreciate it.

Rabbi Meir says: "Whoever engages in the study of Torah for its own sake achieves many things. Moreover, it was worth creating the world for his sake alone. He is called 'a friend, a beloved, a lover of God, a lover of people'" or, in a more precise translation, "a lover of all creatures," which is an all-embracing concept. It includes everything from angels to vermin. To be such a person requires much more than being a mere "lover of humanity." The Mishna continues: "a joy to God, a joy to humanity" – or, in a better translation: "he makes God glad, he makes creatures glad."

And what does the Torah do for him? Torah "clothes him with humility and reverence, and equips him to be righteous, saintly, upright and faithful. It keeps a person far from sin, and draws him near to virtue."

This description of what Torah study does to a person's character doesn't say much about intellectual achievement. Rather, it speaks about the human being. Indeed, in Jewish law, someone who is a gifted scholar but does not behave properly is considered a despicable human being. The Talmud calls a person who is merely erudite "a book-carrying donkey," or "a basket full of books." Carrying books rather than, say, straw, does not make a donkey any less a donkey.

So Torah study must transform the student's personality. If it does not, then there is something wrong with the teacher, the teaching method, or the pupil himself. In fact, the Mishna goes on to say that while Torah *equips* a person to be righteous and pious and honest and faithful etc., it does not actually *make* him so. It creates the possibility, prepares the ground. No one will ever become anything unless he wants to; but the right conditions must be provided. To prepare the ground means to take care not just of what people *know*, but also of what they *make* of that knowledge.

The Mishna goes on to describe some of the rewards or results of learning: "It endows the student with sovereignty and authority, the power of keen judgment. The secrets of Torah are revealed to him, he becomes a burgeoning fountain, a never-ending stream; he becomes modest and patient, forgiving of insult." The Mishna exalts him over all of creation.

This is a magnificent description of a Torah scholar, and whenever it is realized, such a scholar not only has a halo around him, but shines with a bright light.

As we said, this description touches on almost every possible aspect – except for intellectual achievement. And yet the Talmud – which nowadays is the most central part of Torah study – is a highly intellectual pursuit. Furthermore, most Torah study is not about morality or sanctity. It is about litigation, laws of purity, sins and crimes of various kinds, etc. And the Torah scholar knows it all. And yet, what it makes of him is, ideally, described above.

Why?

The point is that character education is not achieved through direct exhortation such as "be nice," "be honest," etc. Children are very clever. They observe their teachers from every possible angle. It is extremely difficult to fool them. Whatever the subject being studied, what the teacher transmits about character is what the teacher actually is. The teacher is the model, so you have to be what you teach. When a teacher is a fake, the students will know it right away.

Thus, for instance, a teacher must be able to say "I don't know." The importance of this cannot be over-stressed. Pretending knowledge undermines not only the knowledge, but the character of the pupils. Sometimes it is much better to say: Dear pupils, I myself am far from perfect in this point; so while I am teaching you, I myself am also trying to make some progress.

Beyond being fair and honest, this approach will be respected by the children, because they will feel that they and their teacher are going somewhere together. For how many among us can really say to our pupils: "Look at me, and behave exactly like this"?

Certain things are taught only by example. A teacher, by definition, is a role model, and when a teacher has humility and integrity, these qualities are transmitted. They are transmitted not only by personal example, but also by the teacher's demands. Many teachers create dishonesty, intellectual or otherwise, by their demands, as well as by what they give the better marks for – for instance, by giving a good mark to a dishonest paper just because it is "nice."

But there is more to it than that. It says here that Torah learning "endows him [the learner] with sovereignty and authority," or in other words, the knowledge of what it means to master something, and what it means not to master something. Mastery means that one becomes the owner, the boss, of what is studied. Lack of mastery is reflected in the sloppiness that comes from not understanding what it means to do something, anything, properly. Learning the proper way of doing things may be a student's most important acquisition.

Whether a teacher manages to cover all the material in the curriculum – or more, or less – is not all that significant. But if a teacher succeeds in teaching children how to do things properly, that is an achievement. With time, such pupils will be able to close any gap. To create a fine human being, even if that human being has less formal education than the average student in another school – that is truly worthwhile.

Let me conclude with a story: In Jerusalem, there is a teachers' seminary that in its first years was a very good school. The teachers there were some of the greatest scholars in Jerusalem at the time, and Jerusalem is a town with a fair number of scholars. Years later, I asked a number of graduates of that school which person had the greatest impact on them. Interestingly enough, many said it was the charlady – a little Yemenite woman with no formal education. Whenever they had a real problem, they didn't go to any of the teachers, nor to the principal. They went to get this woman's advice.

Few people – teachers included – have real knowledge. In terms of knowledge, most teachers are not qualitatively different from their students, only quantitatively different – small ignoramuses vs. bigger ignoramuses. It is people like that char lady who are most needed in schools; because it is that kind of people who really matter. All the rest are forgotten.

To sum up: a good teacher is one who helps his student learn how to learn, and who teaches him to become a *mentsch*. This is the greatest possible achievement of any teacher. Whoever does that, does something God-like, for he has created a human being.

Chicago, 17 November 1997

Chapter Twenty-Two

Boundaries of Holiness

Any deliberation on holiness is superfluous – or altogether impossible. The one who knows and feels doesn't need to discuss it; and the one who doesn't know cannot be made to know. One cannot describe the nature of color to a blind person, while he who sees can comprehend color on his own.

Still, it is possible to speak of defining the boundaries, to define boundaries in a way that will be meaningful even to those who do know. And therefore I shall say a few words about that which probably should not be spoken.

I will begin with a distinction made many generations ago between "holiness" and "the holy." One possible definition might be that holiness is the essence, the base of the matter. The holy is all that touches upon holiness, all that imbibes from holiness, or relates to holiness. Because, after all, there is holiness itself, and there is that which becomes holy because it is related to holiness.

Many books have been written about holiness, and they all face one fundamental dilemma – how can one speak about the unspeakable? This is the quandary of mystics, sometimes of philosophers and even of artists. One definition that carries a large measure of truth is that holiness is that which is found beyond all boundaries, that which reaches infinity and absolute transcendence. Our perception of holiness can be expressed by the term (used also by Freud) "an oceanic feeling."

A sensitive person standing on the seashore faces something grand and immeasurable, something infinite. Similarly, I would suggest that this feeling of "me and infinity" is the basic sensation of one who stands before holiness. This definition is imperfect, since the "oceanic feeling," like the ocean itself, is finite. Our perception of infinity is in many ways an attempt to perceive the unperceivable, to understand that which cannot be understood – that which is, in essence, unattainable by its very definition.

Any attempt to enter the realm of holiness is paradoxical. Because I have entered it, then it is not truly holy; and if it is truly holy, I shall always stand outside it. The reply to Moses' request to see the face of God, is: "You cannot see My face, for there shall no man see Me and live…and you shall see My back parts, but My face shall not be seen" (Exodus 33:20–23).

This indeed is the point: it is impossible to see the Face; at most, we can achieve an indirect, "lateral" recognition, but never a direct fundamental view.

And on a second level, from holiness come the holy things, those things that are touched by holiness or inspired by it. Here it is possible to speak of levels, of degrees, of inner holiness and external holiness, of the Holy of Holies and of other Holy entities. Here there are boundaries, levels and things to which we can relate. But the starting point must still be remembered – the holy is that which relates to holiness.

This reminder is especially important because the concept of holiness, like many other things, has undergone a process of reduction and diminution over time. Now holiness is ascribed to all kinds of worldly things: holiness of labor and holiness of the right to strike, holiness of the Supreme Court and of the State, of the Israel Defense Forces, and more – a world full of holinesses.

It must be said that this multiple use of the word "holiness" is not only secularization. When I take the concept of "holiness" and ascribe to it things that are not holy, it is actually a process of secularization. But another aspect of the process, which is possibly even worse, is that it is a cheapening of the concept.

When "holiness" becomes everything of importance or significance, or everything worthy of attention, this is degradation. It doesn't really matter what is being termed "holy" – it is always a cheapening of the term. This debasement does not only break the term into small pieces, it damages its very essence, so that the imagined "holy" loses any association to actual holiness.

This calls for a pun from the Hebrew language. The degraded *kadosh* ("holy"), becomes *kadesh* (slang: a prostitute). And things to which the title of holiness is unduly attached become a pile of "*kadesh*" – cheapened because of this cheap, degrading, uncontrolled use of holiness, something which should have been untouchable.

Examination of the boundaries of holiness raises a fundamental question that my acquaintance with Adi made me realize actually exists, though I don't know if it has a complete solution. Holiness is infinite; any glimpse of it means breaking through its boundaries, from outside the realm, outside the system. And the question is – is it possible to stand on the periphery of holiness, and yet remain within its bounds? Is it possible to be on the threshold of holiness?

Is it not a matter of either being inside – and then I am in an entirely different reality – or being outside?

It is also possible to raise this question in a more comprehensive and specific way. Doesn't the very fact that I am encountering holiness necessarily mean that all other values become nullified, meaningless? For coming in contact with holiness can be likened to infinity in mathematics – in relation to infinity, everything else is zero.

And the question is: Is holiness concerned with anything other than itself? Is holiness concerned with things such as science, politics, society and beauty? Is holiness, by its very characterization, not self-defining, self-sufficient, a negation of all other entities? Because, in actuality, that which is holy necessarily goes beyond all bounds and definitions, turning everything else into zero.

For those who have any contact with holiness, this is no trivial matter. This is not a problem for one who creates Ḥanukka lamps, or one who draws "Jewish" pictures. The problem begins on the other side: Can one who has touched holiness avoid being totally burnt? Aaron's sons, who entered holiness, came out – as our sages describe it – with a "burnt soul and an intact body." The entrance into holiness is a dead-end with a sort of warning attached – "Everything burns!" "Everything" means things like a homeland, a family, life; all of these must, almost by definition, be nullified against infinity.

Not all those who enter holiness come out in peace. Nonetheless, when speaking of holiness, of its boundaries and values, it is possible to speak about it, not from the vantage point of those who are inside, but from the vantage point of those who are outside. They are looking in from a distance. Sometimes it is a distance of yearning, sometimes of dread, and sometimes it is a distance of an emotion that often prevails among the more sensitive in our midst: if I get too close, I shall never be able to come out, I shall never be able to remain what I am. Maybe I shall not be able to survive at all.

This is the reason why there are people, good people among them, who have a phobia about holiness, just because they are so strongly attracted to it. They stand before holiness yet keep a distance from it, in a sort of struggle. There are people who escape holiness by running in the opposite direction. They pursue the mundane in order to avoid the temptation of holiness, which perhaps is the greatest temptation of all, as well as the greatest threat. One goes out, behaves wildly, exults, becomes drunk, or philanders, only to avoid any contact with the temptation – or the threat – of holiness.

Yet there are still people who observe holiness with a great degree of longing; their difficulty is with what perhaps cannot be referred to as connecting points, but is nevertheless points of contact. Because in a certain way holiness is, in essence, similar to what is known in chemistry as "noble elements" – elements that never mix with others, never become a part of compounds, but can still be touched. So when a person touches holiness, even only superficially, and wishes to create for that holiness a sanctuary of some kind, a problem arises: How can one confine holiness, represent it, or give it space, in a way that can be perceived by human beings?

One of the loftiest universal prayers in the Bible is the blessing

King Solomon delivered at the inauguration of the Temple (1 Kings, ch. 8). His statement is a clear verbalization of this dichotomy: "The Lord said that He would dwell in the thick darkness. I have surely built You a House to dwell in, a settled place for You to abide in forever."

God decided to dwell in the thick darkness, and thus it should be. He is within the unknowable, the indescribable, the limitless, as it says in that same prayer (ibid. verse 27): "Behold, the heaven and heaven of heavens cannot contain You, how much less this House that I have built."

When I am facing heaven and the heaven of heavens, I am standing on the side, distant and separate – yet the house I am building should be the place of the holy, not a house for holiness.

For holiness will never be confined in a house or closed in by a fence – not within the limits of our galaxy or anywhere within our cosmos. It cannot be held within anything at all. Yet we can try to create a place for the holy, for those things that derive from holiness, those things that resonate with holiness. And those things that resonate with holiness are what we can term truly holy. They have acquired something from the attribute of holiness because they are sensitive to it, they know it and recognize it. And it is in those things that are holy that we can speak about bonds.

Every mathematician knows that an otherwise correct mathematical formula that is not elegant has something wrong with it. In other words, in a field that has no connection with the concept of beauty per se, there is a working definition of "inelegant formulas," and a formula that is not elegant is flawed. This, then, is a slightly strange approach to truth and beauty. It is not a sphere of visual esthetics or philosophy, and yet things that contain true values do have some kind of relationship to beauty.

It turns out that, although truth is not examined in terms of beauty, its boundaries, its definition, and its correct presentation do bear a relationship to beauty. This is somewhat similar to the attitude toward the holy (note: toward the holy, not toward holiness). For holiness, there is no standard of measurement, no measuring stick. For holiness, there is no way to build a network of values, borders or definitions. But for whatever lies between us and holiness, definitions can be created.

And so the holy – that which stands at the point of contact

between holiness and reality – must be in harmony with many things. It must be in harmony with concepts such as truth, honesty, morality, reality, and even beauty. The holy, when it appears, when it reveals itself, must be beautiful. The holy does not need beauty as an ornament; but beauty is part of the harmony of its being. This beauty is well defined. It is also complex, because it stands at the meeting point between holiness per se and beauty per se. And yet there is some point at which these two things can somehow interconnect.

Let me finish with a verse that, however simple, is quite enigmatic: "*Zeh Keli ve'anvehu*, This is my God and I will adorn Him" (Exodus 15:2). This verse has two classical interpretations. According to one, *anvehu* is interpreted as *ani vehu*, "I and He," what is known in Latin as *imitatio Dei* – imitating God, being like Him in attributes, in actions, and in other ways. The second interpretation sees *anvehu* as derived from beauty – the commitment is to adorn, to make the holy beautiful.

These two interpretations are not mutually exclusive. In fact, they speak about one and the same thing. When one comes in contact – closely or remotely – with the holy, the holy must somehow emanate upon him. This emanation must find expression in ways that are perfect in terms of other values – in terms of conduct, existence and beauty. When these things join together, I am still on the periphery, within the holy; but perhaps then it is possible to glance at holiness from a distance.

21 February 2002

Chapter Twenty-Three

The Tree of Knowledge and the Tree of Life

Within the ocean of blood and fire that now surrounds us, there are seemingly isolated islands. Here we are, sitting and talking about Torah, mitzvot, and good deeds. On the one hand, it may be comforting to know that there are such islands of serenity. But is it right, at a time like this, to be in a kind of bubble of goodness?

Maimonides (*Mishneh Torah*, Hil. Teshuva 3:6) gives a list of people who do not have a share in the World to Come. This list includes "apostates, skeptics, those who deny the Torah," etc. However, it also includes "he who separates himself from the congregation." This person, says Maimonides, may be flawless in faith and deeds, yet he doesn't want to be part of the Congregation of Israel. He wants no share either in its troubles or in its joys. It is as if he says: "Let me live alone!"

For that reason, such a person has no share in the world to come. He is rejected forever. If we do not wish to be included in that category, we must remember that even the islands of quiet exist within and struggle against the noise of the world around us. Therefore we must not seclude ourselves. Rather, we must always remember that we are living within the current reality, with all its confusion, flames, danger, and blood.

I do not want to speak about politics – not because politics is inherently loathsome; on the contrary, it is part and parcel of our cultural environment. In a place like ours, whoever wants to keep away from politics is to be considered "one who separates himself from the congregation." Yet with all that, I choose to speak about a completely different issue, though one that is profoundly related to what is happening now.

I believe that the foundations of things around us are not always visible. Often they are to be found much deeper, and sometimes they seem totally abstract. So too, the topic about which I am going to speak may seem abstract, but I believe it is deeply connected with our current reality. This connection is not a mystical one; it is the direct link between the blemishes of the mind, heart, and consciousness, and what is happening to us now.

The topic is "sophistication."*

The only place in the Torah in which one may, perhaps, find a similar term is in Genesis 3:1, which says: "The serpent was more subtle than any beast of the field." In contemporary terms I would translate it as, "the serpent was more sophisticated." Indeed, this is what he was. He was neither wise nor clever, but he was sophisticated, the very first sophisticated being.

Defining sophistication is not easy (because any simple definition cannot possibly be fully satisfactory, and any sophisticated definition will necessarily lead – as has happened – to a vicious circle of defining sophistication by means of increasingly sophisticated concepts). I shall therefore not speak about the term itself, nor about the many ways – from storming in to creeping in – whereby it enters our lives. I would like to focus on the fact that sophistication forces the most basic things not only out of our discourse, but even out of the very process of thought.

---

* The Hebrew equivalent, *tiḥkum*, which I dislike at least as much as I abhor the English original, is a relatively new word. Its very existence in Hebrew is surprising, given that Hebrew contains quite a number of synonyms for "wisdom." Obviously, the word was imported into the language to serve as a translation for the English term.

Sophistication demolishes the possibility of conducting a simple conversation, making a simple statement, or touching the fundamentals of existence. The abundance of explanations and points of view that is the hallmark of sophistication, blinds us to the simple knowledge of what is right and what is wrong, what is truth and what is falsehood. We forget the meaning of simple words such as "I hate," and "I love." Instead, we get dragged into a heap of complex, convoluted talk that is completely detached from reality, from genuine experiences and emotions. After sophistication has completed its work, there is no longer a need to deny or ignore the basics. Sophisticated people no longer believe in, or understand, anything.

Consequently, what is most fundamental not only ceases to be self-evident. It becomes totally incomprehensible. I am speaking about basic words such as: "I believe," "I am afraid," "I am a Jew." One can explain these things at great length, with or without footnotes, in complicated sentences that no one understands – for deliberate obfuscation is part of what sophistication is about. Unlike sophistry, sophistication is not an attempt to mislead. Rather, it may be likened to cutting down flowering, fruit-bearing trees, grinding them, turning them into paper, and then replacing them with paper trees and flowers. The sophisticated person converts living things into much more complex, complicated, "wiser" surrogates – and in the process loses touch with the basics.

The curse of sophistication today affects mainly educated people, or those who want to be considered educated. Before becoming sophisticated, a person could go to an exhibition, see a painting, and say, "This is beautiful!" Today, one can no longer say such a thing, just as one can no longer say that something is horrid. Rather, one needs to demonstrate knowledge of the precise era to which this painting belongs, the genre used, and whether it is outdated, modern or post-modern, how this painting relates to the works of other painters, and whether the brush strokes go from right to left or from left to right. After all that, who knows anymore if the thing itself is beautiful or ugly?

This applies also to religion, as well as to an increasing number of religious people. Today, religious people are becoming sophisticated. They speak a highbrow language and write highbrow poetry and literature. They explain Judaism in a metaphysical way and in a kabbalistic way, in a poetic way and in a literary way. All these explanations brush aside the simple reality of speaking and thinking about basic concepts, and of experiencing the most fundamental things.

Sophistication is a deadly poison to Judaism because it eradicates all those things that – even if somewhat "primitive" – are *real*. The sophisticated person no longer has children; he has state-of-the-art dolls (sometimes living ones). He has no life; he has super-modern machinery. All this sophistication creates a complete and self-sustaining structure, which I often encounter in religious life. All the explanations, all the attempts to be bigger and brighter, make us lose our most basic understandings.

This process also occurs with emotions and reactions. We can no longer say about anything: "How good it is!" – just as we can no longer exclaim: "Phooey!" Man has become a captive of this style, this jargon. He has become so elaborate, ornate, and refined that nothing true remains.

These matters are now part of the political discourse in Israel. Without referring to the Right or the Left, I can say only this: before we were sophisticated, we knew there was something called "The land of Israel," whatever it may be. Now that we have become sophisticated, we are no longer aware of its existence. There was a time when we knew there was something called "enemy." Now there is no longer an "enemy." Instead, there is such a profusion of complex, refined terms that we no longer know what an "enemy" is, or who is a "friend."

If we go back to the serpent, we can see that sophistication contains an element that is fundamentally irrelevant. Let us examine the dialogue between the serpent and Eve. Even though the serpent is difficult to describe, it obviously was not a small, simple creature of the reptile family. It was extremely elegant, charming and educated; in short, it was sophisticated. And there was Eve, who, as the Talmud attests, was a beauty, but apparently totally uncultured.

Now, these two have a dialogue. The serpent suggests that Eve eat the fruit, and she replies, in the simplest of terms: "It's forbidden!" But a word such as "forbidden" is so passé! Sophisticated people are no longer familiar with terms such as "forbidden," or "no." So instead of speaking about the issue itself, the serpent starts discussing the motivation of He who forbade: "Yea, has God said you shall not eat" – what was it that made Him say such a thing?

Poor Eve! Prior to that encounter, she knew that some things were permitted and others were forbidden. Now she no longer knows. True, the serpent does not tell her that everything is permitted; but it says: "Look, here is a world that is much more complicated, more sophisticated." And it tempts her to enter this world: "Eat it!"

Indeed, if one looks at how a serpent moves, one can understand what sophistication is. The serpent does not move in a straight line; it is incapable of that. The serpentine way of moving is one of the most beautiful things there is, something between a wave and a dance. But the serpent is a serpent, and it kills. For the fruit – not the fruit of the Tree of Knowledge, but the fruit of the serpent – is death, the total annihilation of human relations, of basic understanding and feeling.

Once upon a time, everyone – simple and intelligent alike – knew that one should awaken and *daven* Shaḥarit. People may not have known why. Nobody provided subtle explanations about the vibrations and metaphysics of the thing; but they knew they had to get up and get moving. Now, people are no longer aware of that, because they are sophisticated. And sophistication kills. On the face of things, sophistication only seems to add more refined structures of thought. If so, why not build these rococo towers even higher? Why not add filigree of thought, the more the better? It turns out, however, that these thought-towers destroy the foundations from which they sprout. They destroy the most basic concepts: "no," "yes," "I am for," "I am against" – all those things that are simple, rudimentary, elementary, perhaps even somewhat foolish – but they are *life*.

Ecclesiastes puts this very succinctly: "A little folly is dearer than wisdom and honor" (Ecclesiastes 10:1). There is grandeur in honor and splendor in wisdom, but both of these may freeze and die due to a lack of inner vitality. "A little folly" – a little simple, naive, innocent emotion: love, fatherliness, compassion – is what endows wisdom and honor with the minute, yet so absolutely necessary, seed of life.

Indeed, what prevented Adam from eating from the Tree of Life? I imagine that the Tree of Life was not more difficult to reach than the Tree of Knowledge. In fact, the two trees may have been adjacent to each other, in the middle of the Garden. But after having eaten the fruit of the Tree of Knowledge, Adam was no longer capable of recognizing the Tree of Life. The Tree of Life may have been right in front of him, but it just didn't occur to him to consider the possibility. He probably thought to himself: "The Tree of Life cannot possibly be this wretched little shrub. It must be something a lot more splendid and sophisticated." He did not reach for the Tree of Life at that moment because he was sure that he had to meditate and read a lot of professional literature first. This is why man is still so far from the Tree of Life.

As I have said before, I do not want to speak about politics, nor about the present. I want to speak about one thing only: the need to reconnect with the basic things, the points of truth that we can grasp, and which are the roots of existence. I mean the simplest things: "good," "bad," "beautiful," "ugly," "I love," "I hate," "this is my homeland," "this is my religion," "this is what should be done." I know that these concepts are not in fashion these days. Nevertheless, if we want to live, let us come before the curse of the serpent befalls us – and hold on to the Tree of Life.

12 October 2000

About the Author

Rabbi Adin Steinsaltz is a teacher, philosopher, social critic, and prolific author who has been hailed by *Time* magazine as a "once-in-a-millennium scholar." His lifelong work in Jewish education earned him the Israel Prize, his country's highest honor.

Born in Jerusalem in 1937 to secular parents, Rabbi Steinsaltz studied physics and chemistry at the Hebrew University. He established several experimental schools and, at the age of twenty-four, became Israel's youngest school principal.

In 1965, he began his monumental Hebrew translation and commentary on the Talmud, and completed it in 2010. The Rabbi's classic work of Kabbala, *The Thirteen Petalled Rose*, was first published in 1980 and now appears in eight languages. In all, Rabbi Steinsaltz has authored some sixty books and hundreds of articles on subjects ranging from zoology to theology to social commentary.

Continuing his work as a teacher and spiritual mentor, Rabbi Steinsaltz established a network of schools and educational institutions in Israel and the former Soviet Union. He has served as scholar-in-residence at the Woodrow Wilson Center for International Studies in Washington, DC and the Institute for Advanced Studies at Princeton

About the Author

University. His honorary degrees include doctorates from Yeshiva University, Ben Gurion University of the Negev, Bar Ilan University, Brandeis University, and Florida International University.

Rabbi Steinsaltz lives in Jerusalem. He and his wife have three children and many grandchildren.

The fonts used in this book are from the Arno family

Other works by Adin Steinsaltz
available from Maggid

Biblical Images

The Candle of God

The Thirteen Petalled Rose

The Essential Talmud

The Tales of Rabbi Nachman of Bratslav

Talmudic Images

Teshuvah

Change and Renewal

Maggid Books
The best of contemporary Jewish thought from
Koren Publishers Jerusalem Ltd.